KEYS TO CREATIVE WRITING

Activities to Unlock Imagination in the Classroom

GERALD FLEMING

Marina Middle School
San Francisco

Allyn and Bacon
Boston   London   Toronto   Sydney   Tokyo   Singapore

Library of Congress Cataloging-in-Publication Data

Fleming, Gerald J., 1946–
    Keys to creative writing : activities to unlock imagination in
the classroom / Gerald J. Fleming.
        p.   cm.
    "Portions of this book appeared in Seeds flying in a fresh light,
© 1988 . . ."—T.p. verso.
    Includes bibliographical references and index.
    ISBN 0-205-12892-0
    1. English language—Composition and exercises—Study and
teaching (Elementary) 2. Creative writing (Elementary
education) 3. Creative thinking—Study and teaching.
I. Fleming, Gerald J., 1946–   Seeds flying in a fresh light.
II. Title.
LB1576.F475   1991
372.6'23—dc20   90-20242
                                                                   CIP

Printed in the United States of America
10 9 8 7 6 5 4 3 2 1   95 94 93 92 91

For the real heroes —
the kids who wake themselves,
get dressed (same clothes),
have breakfast (no breakfast),
and come to school.

Contents

CONTENTS

CONTENTS

Preface

I'm thinking of the teacher with thirty-five kids. Eighteen of the kids are reading and writing far below grade level. Of those, five are behavior problems.

I'm thinking of the teacher with thirty-eight gifted kids. They're voracious, hungry for new knowledge and ideas and work that interests them—work that allows for their particular *selves* to shine through.

I'm thinking of the teacher new to the teaching of writing, the teacher feeling stuck doing the same old things each year, the teacher who may not teach middle school but who may want to stimulate her high school or community college or senior citizen group toward the excitement of writing.

Although they aim for middle school level, the activities in this book serve all these groups. The ideas are not necessarily original or exhaustive; they simply *work*. Guaranteed!

The ideas herein will engage students, will loosen and let flow their writing skills, will build confidence, push limits, and—perhaps most importantly—if used regularly, implant in students the idea that writing is not only integral as a means of communication, but also integral to the self.

It is my hope especially that this book will succeed in serving teachers in transition, schools in transition, and "teachers in the workshop."

The teacher-in-transition (perhaps you?) is the colleague whose class size, already relatively low, allows for the *possibility* of a fully developed writing workshop at least three days a week. But the idea of *creative writing* is still a bit undefined for that teacher, a bit nervous-making. There needs to be an intermediate step. The teacher needs to know that there is firm ground under that tentative step.

The school—or district—in transition (perhaps yours?) is one that still believes that class size makes no difference in learning, and whose teachers, knowing full well how long the crawl toward enlightenment might take, continue to watch in astonishment as *more* and *more* students surge into their rooms at the beginning of each period. They know the meaning of exhaustion, these teachers, and teach valiantly despite such conditions.

"Teachers in the workshop" (you?) already have a fully and smoothly functioning routine going in their classrooms. They simply need a fresh idea now and then to help along kids who are stuck, or they need books full of writing ideas placed conspicuously at their students' disposal.

Finally, this book seeks the hands of those teachers comfortable with adapting activities downward or upward in grade, either according to their particular and often wildly asymmetrical classes or according to actual grade levels. Though aimed at middle school, work in this book has been used well in elementary, senior high, and community college classes.

Kids write well—when the topics are interesting, and when there's *room to move and change* inside those topics. It is my hope that this book serves its purpose by making the kind of writing herein important to your curriculum, and by finally engendering in students a commitment to an ultimate goal: sustained, independent writing.

"Mrs. Williams—want to see a story I wrote over the weekend?"

Acknowledgments

I have many people to thank for the existence of this book.

San Francisco School District teachers Deloris Blount, Larry Prager, and Mary Ann Wold contributed ideas. Marilyn Stepney, Don Melsopp, and Ruthmary Cordon encouraged and supported the project.

Also, the following writers were of great help, either in giving energy to the project or in offering their own poignant ideas and insights: Ellery Akers, Duane BigEagle, Miriam DeUriarte, Bill Edmondson, Russell Edson, Peter Kunz, Genny Lim, Robbie Long, Devorah Major, Gail Newman, Carol Lee Sanchez, and Judith Serin.

The writers whose works appear in the Selected Bibliography have influenced me greatly, and I hope that your attention one day will grace their books as well.

My daughter, Jessica, has influenced me, too. In uncountable ways she has shown me how to see.

Thanks to the San Francisco Education Fund's Gladys Thatcher and to Barbara Ustanko for their support of an earlier version of "How to Produce a School Literary Magazine."

Thanks to Superintendent Ramon Cortines, Wendy Coyle, and Dorothy Erlich for contributing to the symposium on censorship.

Deep gratitude goes to the students whose writings appear in these pages. *You taught me.*

My friend David Hoffman reminds me that many years ago our son Gabe, then a kindergartner, said: *"There are a lot of things invisible in the world, but we don't know how many, because we can't see 'em!"* Thanks, Gabe. These words could be the motif for this book.

Finally, thanks to my wife, Gerry, for continuing to live with me (knock on wood!).

CHAPTER ONE

Introduction: Some Thoughts for Teachers

We *live in strange times.* Could these have been the first words from the caveman's mouth? Certainly much of written history attests that anyone living any time thinks upon his own time as strange.

But this feeling of strangeness holds a beauty, for it allows us to stand back, make ourselves distant, and watch the world in its elaborate configurations and choreographies.

If we stand back today—say, over there—there in the corner of that classroom, or this one, or this one . . . what do we see?

We see teachers still riding the huge wave whose name is *Back to Basics.* We see teachers, still underpaid and unheralded, struggling to give kids the tools society dictates are important. Some of these importances remain constant over the years. Some change with the political climate.

In today's upper-level English classes, a teacher benevolently aspires to impart skills of grammar, comprehension of reading, of spelling, vocabulary, survival writing skills, basic literate writing skills, and, if he or she is either gifted or fortunate, "higher" abilities such as the love of good literature and the creation of fine writing.

The *standardized test* looms in every English teacher's classroom like a larger-than-life beast from a Gary Larson cartoon. There are national tests, state tests comparing schools and districts, local tests assessing specific skills, fancy tests for entry into fancy schools, and minimum-standard tests.

It is inevitable that teachers look at these many tests, and, by the sheer weight of this tool-cum-cudgel, gear what they teach to mesh with the machinery of tests. To an extent, perhaps this is good. But in many ways the result is a profound pedagogic impoverishment.

What happens to *creative writing* in the process?

The answers seem to be:

1. In classrooms, the frequency of creative writing work diminishes.
2. Creative writing is relegated to the "luxury" category.
3. The very definition of *creative writing* changes.

Certainly, many teachers use a wide variety of dynamic, interesting writing techniques as a crucial part of their work. It is my sense, though, that many more teachers have lost sight of what constitutes *creative* writing and what energies inform it. Today's predictable "Creative Writing" project is most often a paragraph or essay with a cute title; "What I Did During Summer Vacation" has been replaced with "My Favorite Pair of Socks."

By all means, expository work is important, but is it not important as *part* of a well-balanced writing regimen? A person *needs* to be able to write a sentence, a paragraph, and a decent short essay. But when a student is exposed only to such, she or he, unless exceptionally gifted or tenacious, will come to regard such work as a kind of literary automatic dishwasher: you fill it up (with words), making sure the words are put in the spaces made for them (introductory paragraph, "body," conclusion), close the door and push the button (hand it in), and the stuff comes out clean (corrected, graded, passed). In this sense we are teaching our youth to use words as commodities, each of equal value, sold like tons of pork bellies in the universe of supply and demand.

It's not as simple as that; I know.

But it doesn't seem revolutionary to offer up the idea that one of the goals of literacy ought to be sharp self-expression in words, or *creative writing*, and that this writing ought to have as its *currency* not passage of a course or a grade, but a move toward deeper *understanding*. It is with this in mind—and guided by the idea that *the word* embodies one of the few vehicles available to us as humans with which to express the precision of our thoughts, the amusement in our lives, the width of our dreams, and the depth of our feelings—that this book is made.

Kids enjoy the activities in this book, teachers welcome reading their results, and the happy dilemma on the teacher's part is whether, at the request of students, to repeat a popular activity, or to swim toward new waters.

* * *

5

Teacher: will you be faithful a while longer and stay to consider an opinion on the teaching of this fantastic beast *creative writing?*

I hope so.

We spend so many days with our kids, and within each day are divisions and subdivisions of *who we are* as perceived by those kids.

On Monday we may be the stern grammarian who actually *cares* what an antecedent is: can somehow muster the zeal to stand there so foolishly and talk about indirect objects as if these untouchable objects have some true connection to a teenager's life.

On Tuesday, a different person: the snake-oil salesman trying to coax kids to buy into an essay assignment entitled "The Person I Admire Most"—dancing around at the chalkboard, drawing big circles, little circles, inserting cryptic words into those circles, engaged in the teacher's cult passion for *prewriting.*

For half of Wednesday, a pacing drill sergeant for the armies of prefixes and suffixes and homonyms and antonyms; for the other half, an interrogator whose rubber face at any moment might whirl and grimace in your direction, ask you a question on the content of the reading at hand—and will you know the page? Will you stumble on your words? Will the words even get past the metal bars of your new braces? And how does your hair look?

Maybe Thursday the teacher is the reader of a good book—almost mother-like, father-like. In good, clear tones, she or he is reading a story you love. And you love the voice on those days—how it soothes you—and the classroom is a safe place—warm—and you wish those times would never end.

Friday the persona changes radically, and the teacher has become automatic, firing Spelling Words at you, or dictating sentences. He is a human made of iron who banishes a disruptive child from the class, then continues. But though you secretly are glad, though the absence of this class dunce is welcomed and peace again reigns and the dictation proceeds, the controlled anger of the teacher still fills the room, and the judgmental taskmaster is completely unapproachable. You'd better wait until Monday to ask for that Kleenex.

Such a specter!

And though, really, it's less than that, and more than that, I propose that on days we do creative writing work with kids we consciously adopt a different self, and pretend that our own good friends have asked us, since we're good teachers, to spend some time with them and guide them through some interesting (and yes, let's say it— *painless*) writing activities.

So we're relaxed. We might even have on more casual clothes. We're *accepting*. Some didactic judgment remains—enough to control the class—but most falls away.

We have no compulsion toward creating a product. A "product" might occur, but that would be a happy phenomenon. If no fireworks occur, that's O.K., too. A teacher engaged in *process* is not a lazy teacher, though at times creative writing work goes so smoothly and effortlessly that one feels almost guilty for not "working harder." (Read: interfering.)

We must remember, as teachers, as *guides*, that writing *is* process—and not always product.

Many times, when we involve ourselves in process, what we hoped for doesn't work out. Think of the last ten times you've made that thing called *dinner*. How many of the ten turned out to your expectations? How many photographs must a photographer take to get one that embodies the elements he desires? How many paintings in a year does a painter make that satisfy her?

So by this measure, we can understand, and admire, and forgive, and congratulate our young writers.

Perhaps your classroom has become a writing workshop in the manner described so saliently by Nancie Atwell in her book *In the Middle* (see the bibliography). If so, then by now you know well the essence of *process*, and the book whose words your eyes now scan will be used, I hope, as a simple adjunct to that dynamism.

* * *

Has that term *creative writing* bothered you for years? It has me. It's so dandified, so imprecise. Some say all writing is creative. It's true that all writing is *made*. But not all writing is created freely, in an environment where subject matter and choice of words and form are all O.K.

But let's attack this issue.

There are many different kinds of writing kids are *expected* to do. In most schools—at the writing of this book, at least—they're *expected* to write book reports or other summaries of reading. They're expected to "write" assigned projects, such as reports on the life of Abe Lincoln or on the civilization of the Incas; they're *expected* to write expositorily on many different *assigned* subjects.

This sense of expectation is a trap for them and for us, because most often such assignments eliminate completely any sense of spontaneity, creativity, or *room to move* inside a particular topic. We collect papers, and we read what we expect to read: deadly boring stuff, controlled, desiccated, predictable, generic.

Boring for us? What must it have been for the student who put pen to paper to "create" it?

In a letter, the writer Ellery Akers shared with me a few thoughts on the nature of *creative writing:*

> *"Last summer we went to the beach on our vacation. It was a special place, and we had fun."*

> This is expository writing. It's perfectly O.K., but it doesn't come out of any need, urgency, or drive. It feels as if it's been prodded out of the student by some English requirement. It doesn't have uniqueness, or personal energy. You've read it before, and will again. Anyone could have written it, not just the particular kid who did. It's inter-

changeable with another kid's work. Lifeless as wilted lettuce.

And this is creative writing:

"Every time I looked at Kelly's face
I got lost in the freckles, like I was lost
in space. They reminded me of clusters
of stars, and whole big galaxies, and
nebulae, and sun spots, which is really
what they were. I told her that, and she
liked it, I think. That was how we got
together, and that's why she'll always be
'the star woman' to me."
— Luis Cernada

This has life, energy, and zing. It
could not have been written by anyone
else but Luis Cernada; it has the blue-
print of his soul. It's personal; it's
unique. No one but Luis could have seen
or felt that about his girlfriend Kelly. It's
something that emerged from his values,
visions, past, raw emotions, and it
couldn't be reproduced by anyone else
who didn't have Luis's particular set of
experiences, loves, and hates. It's
original.

Creative work has zing. It's personal, energetic, alive. It's unique. When
you go to a museum, you can pick out
the Matisses because no one but Matisse
saw and felt like that. He had a kind of

signature *that became instantly recognizable, and we all do, in a way, when we work in a creative vein.*

Akers knows, as we classroom troglodytes know, that expository prose can have its own excellence and glory. But alas, in the classroom, certainly as in life, the *creative* takes a beating at the hands of mundane and expected *realistic prose.*

Dare I say that most assignments given by teachers (as opposed to chosen by students) not only are prose, but are on topics we'd define as "realistic"?

- Discuss someone you regard as a real-life hero.
- What should society do about the cocaine problem?
- What rights should students have in privately owned shopping malls?

You recognize the kind of topic I'm referring to. It's assigned frequently and often even appears in standardized tests. It allows for some individuality, but in my mind's eye I still see around each topic a cyclone fence: close or distant. (Does anyone else want to take these topics and twist them around, creating, say, an essay whose prompt instructs: *Discuss someone you regard as a real-life hero sandwich . . . ?* Kids want to do this too—they naturally want to bring life into death, to muck up with juicy bacteria the sterile environment of academia.)

Call it flight (as opposed to fight, perhaps), call it escape, call it unrealistic, naive, primitive, or pollyannish;

11

but what seems to me important are not only the abilities to define the present world and offer solutions to our multitude of dilemmas, but also the ability to *undefine, fly,* leave reality altogether and create something preposterous and joyful and unexpected and impractical and maybe difficult, but certainly new.

In all of the activities of this book, therefore, there is room to move, and an open invitation to kids: *Change it! Make it yours!*

In his book *Writing the Australian Crawl,* the poet Willam Stafford said that "writing itself is one of the great, free human activities. There is scope for individuality, and elation, and discovery, in writing. For the person who follows with trust and forgiveness what occurs to him, the world remains always ready and deep. . . ."

And this ready, deep world abides lifelong for the student who learns to write creatively.

Setting the Tone/Laying Down the Rules/Establishing a Routine

I think it's a good idea to have the kids make a simple writing folder at the beginning of the term. I pass out full-size, light-colored construction paper, pass out crayons (sharing O.K.), have the kids fold the paper in half and design the cover any way they wish. ("I don't care what you draw, as long as it's not obscene." "I don't care if you can't draw—I can't either!—make a design if you don't want to make a picture." "You'll have to look at this folder all [year] [semester] [quarter]—make something you like to look at!") Just make sure the kids' names are written legibly on the front.

Their work is kept in the folder, and the folder doesn't go home until the end. No lost work, no lost folders.

Alan Ziegler (author of the wonderful book *The Writing Workshop;* see bibliography) doesn't let kids throw anything away. You know the type—the Paper Crumplers. Ziegler maintains that what they've written might be good, or at least some of it might be valuable, to be used perhaps elsewhere. I agree; even if only one line is good, one-line poems can be very powerful!

So: the kids are in the room. You're relaxed. You say something like, "Let's just take it easy today and do some fun writing." Or, "Let's do some easy work today." (That's a ruse, of course; once they get going they'll be working hard, indeed.) Or, "Kids always like it when we

13

do this activity together . . ." (Even if you've never tried it before!)

Then, for the first few such writing sessions, having already established a more accepting persona and an atmosphere of lightness, you relax the kids even further:

"Now don't worry about grades on this. I won't be grading this work in the normal way. We're exploring here. *All learning.* No grades on any of these. All I require is that you try: *do* the activity."

Two things here. First is that you won't need to keep repeating the "no grades" dictum after a few times. The kids will be able to identify such sessions, and progressively will loosen (verbally—not behaviorally) as the year goes on. Second, it's assumed that by now you've established a certain level of minimum commitment ("trying"), and that level doesn't include letting kids play cards, listen to headphones, or come without the simple and necessary tools for writing: paper and pencil. No matter what the activity, the student is to be "on task." (In some activities, periods of quiet thinking are indeed "on task"; in others, noisy group work is, too, if it's also on subject!)

You've gotten an activity from this book, or from another, or from the thousand-volume encyclopedia inside your head. If it's an activity whose level seems to be energetic (say, "Recipe for an Enemy"), you're energetic in the introduction of it. If it's a calmer one, more pensive ("Letter from a Soldier"), you're low-key and pensive as well.

A little brainstorming to get the juices flowing is great. It needn't be long. Kids can talk for only five minutes

14

or so, and in that short time spread energy and understanding. Two kids talking about the experiences of soldiers they've known can do more in two minutes than an hour of adult windbagging!

Now the teacher hones in on the activity, talking about it, and reading examples other kids have written, if some are available.

The examples given can be crucially important. Some kids just don't "get" an abstract, conceptual explanation—but if by way of example you read a real work done by a real kid, you can almost physically see the light bulbs coming on in the kids' brains, and the faces begin smiling.

And in the beginning, the inevitable questions: "Can we print?" (Yes! The idea is to get 'em to write most comfortably!) "Can we use pencil?" (Of course! This is a draft! And no white-out allowed for those manic liquid-eraser types!) *"Does it have to be real?"* (No! No! What is written in any such session can be true, only partly true, or completely fictional.)

This last, I think, is important to emphasize at every session, for the very idea of such license is a thought-loosener, a word-loosener. Kids need to know that Maria, for instance, may not really have said that to her mother, or that Derek may not really think those strange thoughts about hamsters. So much can be taught about the dynamics of *fiction* in reinforcing this license!

Now the kids *write.* It's not easy to write on command: not for everyone, I think. That page is so white, so huge. (Sometimes I have kids scrabble random words at the top just to alter the overwhelming virgin white.) So give them the benefit of the doubt for a while—allow some pondering time.

Some teachers and writers would disagree with this, arguing that it interrupts concentration, but I've found it successful to circulate in the classroom for *two minutes* or so at the beginning of an activity, and coach. To use the "Letter from a Soldier" example: "Aha! Someone's writing a letter from a soldier in Vietnam! Here's another one from a soldier in ancient Greece! And a new idea— here's one from a soldier in the year 2788! There's some exciting work going on here."

Then I think it's good to shut up for as long as possible—as long as kids are working. You might confer individually, whispering (a holy ritual is going on— whispering shows respect!) with a kid who may have run into a roadblock. But silence here yields golden rewards.

Certainly, despite your urging not to worry about spelling at this point—*just get the words down*—some nervous student simply will not be able to continue until he gets you to spell a word. Here, instead of interrupting the entire class, I find it's better nonchalantly to scribble it on the board.

Regarding grammar and spelling, it seems perfectly fine not to worry about these during that first draft. Spelling can—and should—be fixed later. Syntax should be fixed only when problems get in the way of *sense*, or when embarrassment might be caused the writer either in an oral reading or in eventual publication. But certainly much beautiful writing is born in phrases and sentences whose construction is a little "screwy"! Meddlers beware! It's a fine line between fixin' the diction and wreckin' the writing!

Titles? I tell my kids—in most assignments—that titles can come later—after the first or second drafts are finished. *Then you know what it was about.* A title written beforehand in anything but an essay can be a tyranny, and can push the writing toward a prestated direction the student may not want to travel. Later seems better, but some kids become *extremely* nervous when they don't have a title to top the page from the start. So let them; they can always change it later if they want.

What *are* appropriate titles? These days, writers are titling their works from so many different perspectives it's absolute titular anarchy. I've included an appendix that lists fifty titles culled randomly from a few literary magazines I have on hand. Ranging from "Hood Ornament" to "The Corporal Who Stabbed Archimedes," they're wild and fun, and would be great just to read to the kids as a loosening— as yet another way to say, "It's O.K.!"

A final word on titles. Kids don't have much fun when they're asked to title their work after an exercise, like "Indefinite Pronoun Poem," or "Alliteration." They can come up with something better, and there's no reason not to work together on titles. We're involved in process!

17

The Censor—What Not to Let Kids Write

There are some things not to allow, but they are few—very few.

Foul language? "Bathroom humor"? (I love that phrase—it makes me think that jokes exist about tile grout and towels and dandruff shampoo.) In my classes it's O.K. for kids to use some vulgarity, *but* such language should be in the context of the story, dialogue, and so forth, and shouldn't be excessive—i.e., used for the sake of using it, or for being more foul than the kid in the next chair. I tell the kids that we're *sharpening* language, and that in most situations profanity simply isn't necessary.

Of course, in dialogue or in other works that reflect human thought or speech, some profanity certainly will arise. To squelch it is to squelch accuracy. We don't want that. But if, *ahead of time*, your kids know what your expectations are regarding profanity, you won't have any problem. And if by chance a student gets up and begins reading a truly offensive diatribe, you're the boss—stop him and tell him why in the language of a teacher of writing.

What else might not be allowed?

I don't let students write about *each other* in any negative way. This kind of attack can be mortifying to the subject, and is inappropriate in a classroom. I urge kids not to write at all about other kids in the class or even other kids in the school, and not to name staff members negatively. Everyone should feel safe—safe from slander, from defamation, and even from the least embarrassment. Everyone.

That's about it, though. If a kid wants to complain about school, conditions, friendship, home . . . the whole field seems fine.

And what if the kids write an awful lot of depressing stuff—should you lighten the presentations, veer away from such heavy activities?

I think not. Remember that in writing we're asking kids to *be themselves,* and we all know that the self of a child includes its share of heaviness. Indeed, *you* may be the teacher who for the first time has offered that child the chance to express such things—to form those murky feelings into specific thoughts, to *let go.* So let it go.

Once in a great while a student will write something so specific and revealing and plaintive that it can only be recognized as a cry for help. You've seen these—we've all had them. In these instances, it's my belief that all concerns of *art* and *poetic license* be laid aside, and that as a teacher you do what you must do: help. First to the kid, then to the counselor. The safe haven of the written word in a trusted teacher's class in no haven at all if the adult chooses to "respect" its confidentiality, and consequently allows a continuation of abuse, or a self-inflicted death.

But let's lighten our burden now, push away those haunting faces, and talk about something easier, something lyrical.

Rhyme—A Supplication

I wanted to begin these thoughts with something like this:

> *Teachers, please:*
> *(I'm on my knees)*
> *at no time*
> *encourage rhyme.*

But I won't, since such a quatrain, though "cute" in that Dorothy Parkerish American way, might be taken as an unpersuasive argument indeed. And I won't, because I believe in the message of those four lines only ninety-nine of a hundred times.

Please. Though they do like it because they're conditioned to it, discourage rhyming in poetry. Reserve it for songs. Don't stop reading here, friend: I don't want to lose you. Think with me for a while.

Think of all the words in one of those fat Webster's dictionaries. Now think of the sheer number of words you have in your own experience. Now, the deep well of words in the experience of your students. The first is overwhelming, the second immense, the third impressive. What a resource! What tremendous choices!

Now, consider the unfortunate student who, driven by a teacher or a self or peers who demand rhyme, begins her couplet with:

> *You stood there so lightly,*

What *well* does the child go to now? It seems the ending choices she has are: *brightly, nightly, tightly, tritely, politely, sprightly,* and *unsightly.*

Seven choices among many *thousands* of possibilities! Maybe what she really wanted to say was:

> *You stood there so lightly*
> *I wanted to carry you away.*

But what does she end up with?

> *You stood there so lightly*
> *And squeezed my hand so tightly . . .*

This is not what she meant at all! There was no *hand* in the original thought, and less still someone squeezing it! But the hand and the squeezer became necessary accomplices to rhyme.

And that is the crime of rhyme: it sends students away from precision, away from exploring the depth of their meaning—sends them away from the deep waters of Webster's and the lexicon of themselves, and into the shallows, where the trite words live, the predictable words easily snagged and slapped onto the shore of the page. The meaning changes!

But such a change in meaning brings new challenges for the student, no?

Yes—but I submit they are the wrong challenges for kids of this age. Working on a rhyming poem is only

21

half-expressive for teenagers; the other half consists of pure *word puzzle*. We can do better than to give our kids word puzzles to work on during writing time.

But kids want to rhyme, you say, and you're right. Let's also notice, though, that rhyming is done best by certain kinds of kids who may not necessarily be original *writers*, but good *rhymers*. And in the classroom where rhyme reigns, those others—who may be good writers, or at least *undiscouraged* writers—go unrecognized in bitter ignominy.

I do think there are places for rhyme. Kids can write limericks; they can be offered exposure to great songs by Porter or Gershwin or Hart, and can write their own; they can write rhyming lyrics in the pattern of contemporary "hits"; they can write jingles for commercials for products they themselves have invented; they can be taught the form of the ballad, and write moving ones indeed; and they can be exposed to form—to the Shakespearean sonnet, for instance—and learn about *scansion, stress, iambic pentameter*, and *rhyme scheme*, and take a shot at writing their own. So no lack of possibilities for rhymers exists.

But most of the time? I say make statements discouraging rhyme. Kids *can* understand how rhyme imprisons them, if the idea is explained. And the very discussion of rhyme can meld into the important ideas of *rhythm* and *line breaks* in poetry.

You can take a long, crazy run-on sentence you heard somewhere in the hall ("Your hair looks so pretty Patty you're so pretty all those boys come a'runnin I wish

22

I had that hair like you"), write it on the board, and ask the kids to write it as a poem, deciding where *they* think the line breaks should come.

Or, as Alan Ziegler likes, you can do a "cardiogram" at the chalkboard. As you read some expressive passage from a novel or poem, a student can be at the board charting rhythms and stresses the way an EKG machine charts the oscillations of a wild heart.

There's so much! I don't think it's enough to tell kids simply that *very few poets writing today use rhyme, and, after all, you're living today, not yesterday, so* . . . It's better to tell them why rhyme gets in the way, and lead in to the possibilities of line break, meter, stress, rhythm and—who knows?—on a good day, prose poems. (See the appendix for two modern examples of prose poems.)

Response to the Work: What to Say? What to Do?

This is the part for which there are no easy answers. But the *structure* of what we're doing can help us. The nature and quality of response the young writer receives are issues different and wilder in their possibilities than mere presentational techniques. It all can be awesome, even frightening, if we let it. But let's not let it. Again, we're all in *process* here—even the teacher.

A bit about the structure.

There is the "holy" time when the preparation is over and kids are writing. Depending on your teacher-instincts, you either stay in the background—literally in the back of the classroom, out of ready sight—or you gently circulate, helping kids who need a boost, "goosing" their ideas and writing—*their* ideas, not yours, though the temptation is always there to interpose. Here, to use Roger Taylor's jingly phrase, you're the quiet "guide on the side" rather than the "sage on the stage."

O.K. Though a few may still be working, most kids have written, and there's a general sense of completion in the room. Immediacy—tapping into that sweet energy, momentum—is paramount here.

What now? They're done!

Three things, at least:

1. Kids volunteer to read their work; you and the class comment.
2. Kids let other kids orally read their work—they themselves may not want to read, though you gently encourage—and it's O.K. for them to chicken out. Again, comments.
3. After 1 and 2, you collect the papers. You shuffle through them, wax enthusiastic about the quality of the work (you're sincere), say you'd like to read a few anonymously, and ask if there's anyone who *really* does not want his or hers read. You might have given kids the option of scrawling, "Do not read aloud"

across the top of the page. Or you might have established a subtle signal with the class (say, a student raises an index finger to her cheek) and you discreetly scan the class for that signal. This is a privacy you *absolutely* must respect. You read the rest—not these.

Sounds crazy, ritualistic, but only in this overall sense of safety and confidence will your writing class, as a community, flower. (But make a mental note to yourself—set a goal to get those "anonymous" kids to read their own poetry within a few weeks, and a slightly more distant goal for the real recalcitrants.)

Don't get bogged down here. There will be some rotation, depending on the writing activity at hand. Juan might write an intimate, I-don't-want-this-read piece one time, and the next time he might be the first to jump to the front of the room to read his work to the class. And Michelle, who read her crazy poem aloud last time, might prefer that hers not be read aloud at all today.

As a teacher, though, you'll be certain to read these important works privately and carefully, and to make comments either in person or in writing to their authors. Nine times out of ten they want those comments. But do be sensitive for that one who in this assignment wants no comment, and is relieved simply to have said it—to have gotten it out!

What responses to writing are appropriate, and how to go about them? Two categories appear: the first is the way in which we allow for student response—the tone we set, the questions we ask—and the second is the comments we ourselves make.

Informing both of these is the reminder to ourselves: these are kids. Not college students. Not adults. Arguably, their shells are more fragile: sometimes so thin as to be transparent. Even—maybe especially—the tough guys with all their swagger.

In the way we guide student response to work that is read, and in the center from which our own remarks arise, *gentleness* seems the key. Gentleness need not mean absence of excitedness or energy. It's matter of *intent:* no bumping, pushing, or bruising. More like massaging a writer toward a concept or goal.

I think it's perfectly O.K.—and, in many classes, absolutely essential—for the teacher actively to lead discussion among the kids regarding what is read. (In an honors class, once the pattern is set, you'll lead less and less . . .)

Questions like, "What line did you like the best?" "Did Cynthia's [poem, story, letter] give you any feelings?" "How did it make you feel?" "Did anyone think to himself, 'Yeah, that's the way it really is.'?" "At what part did you think that?" "Would you say there's more *showing* here, or *telling*?" "What could she *show* us more of?" "Would you like to see some changes, or is it perfect the way it is?" "What changes would you make?" "Why?" "Does her piece of writing seem to tell the whole story?" "Does your mind say, 'I'm full,' or 'I'm hungry for more'?" "Where would you like to see more details?" "How did you feel about Mr. _____ [character]?" "Did he seem real?" "How could she bring her story to a more complete ending?"

Of course, not all of these typical questions are asked at once—any normal kid would feel overwhelmed. What's certain in these open discussions, though, is that the teacher must:

1. Make clear that there's no popularity contest involved in the discussion of a student's writing. The work is discussed on its own merit. The *work*—not the kid.
2. Make certain that the writer knows that these are *opinions*, and that everyone, notably including the teacher, might be wrong. Repeat this often—kids take glee in it!
3. Make certain that no personal bitterness or attack or derisive laughter is allowed in response to *anyone's* writing. I always insist on this ahead of time, reiterate it, and then, when it occasionally happens anyway, make it a point to bring out the actor in me and go histrionic, launching into an angry *who do you think you are* tirade, bellowing in my best bass voice, gesticulating . . . you get the picture. It makes for unpleasant feelings *that day*, but healing occurs quickly, and you've invested in the future. There is a difference between constructive criticism and mockery; kids know that, and they need for their own creative safety to know that you know it. Kids will be cruel if allowed to be. William Golding didn't lie.

27

A separate subject is the *teacher's* response, both oral and written. When we *listen* to a work being read, we respond not only with the attitude of our bodies (Distracted with something else? Making hand signals to a student across the room? Or in an attitude of concentrated listening?) but also with every sound, every hum and *ooh* and *ahh* that passes our lips.

Do we praise everything? No. Kids know that not all of their work is worthy of praise. They have infallible instincts for phony compliments and empty words.

But do we *encourage* everything? Yes.

I feel strongly that *every* piece of writing a student makes has some salient quality—even if only in a single well-turned phrase. ("I loved how you said his neck was wrinkled like a peach pit—it really gave me a picture of his neck.")

There *is* something good to say about every piece of writing. Say it! ("You wrote a lot more this time, didn't you, Pete.")

But *balance* seems essential, too, as all teachers know. Too much praise can stymie a kid's creativity—keep her forever manufacturing clones of the aboriginal, highly praised work, and away from taking new chances in her writing. And too much negativity, too many layers of "suggestions for improvement," can depress.

Such a hard path it is to walk! While on one hand we want to blend in, immerse ourselves in the support of *process* and *equality*, frequently using phrases like,

"Hmmm . . . let's think about this, everybody . . ," on the other hand the kids know damned well we have *college degrees* and *certificates* and *necks that look like peach pits*, and we know more than they do. That last may or may not be true; but what we *do* know should be shared.

In the right place, though, at the right time.

I think that the *out-loud* part of a writing session is the place primarily of encouragement, of enthusiasm, of eliciting peer response, and of a *few* general and specific teacher's observations, most of which begin with *maybe*, or its tentative cousins.

It is in our *personal conference* and *written* responses we can be more specific, and ought to be. We *do* have expertise—*can* identify lack of development and unintended ambiguities, *do* have the experience to sense where a kid wants to go with a piece, *can* help her go there.

How do we get her there? A tall task: by treating every writing paper before us as if it's the first we've ever seen—pretending that—even when we're weary. By writing (in blue or black ink—not red) a few accepting phrases in the margins, ("I love this." "What a great line!" "Oh, no! I hoped that wouldn't happen to him!") and by being specific without overwhelming the young writer in the sheer volume of a teacher's maniacal specificity.

Some papers might bear only a few comments: "Thanks for sharing this, Sofia. I know it must have been hard to write about"; or, "Michael! Next time more than two words, please!" (This to the new student, first day in your class, on his third school this year, just released from

29

juvenile hall, who with the pencil stub you've provided sullenly scribbles an epithet.)

On certain projects, particular kids can benefit from very specific, detailed ideas on further development. You know those kids. Try to make time to write those comments.

Individual conferences can be equally productive, and often less time-consuming for the overburdened teacher. Not every student has to be conferred with always. I put an asterisk at the top of papers of kids with whom I'd like to meet. It means, "See me—and bring this paper." How it grieves all of us to know how much can be accomplished in these short one-to-one sessions, how large our classes are, how little time.

With small classes, it's quite possible to schedule about five kids per day for conferring. In classes of thirty-five or so, it's *at least* seven days before you make your way to discuss with a particular student what she worked on *last week,* and for her the fiery fuel has diminished, if not evaporated. The knowledge of *this* is what gives us that heavy, sad feeling at the day's end, I think—not simply our physical exhaustion or our salaries.

One last note on response: fancy writing is fine, but don't forget to celebrate simplicity and clarity! This poem, for example,

> *The winds blow the grass*
> *from left to right. The moon shines*
> *night after night with stars.*

is an *almost* haiku written by Ezra Danridge—a kind and tall and tough eighth-grader whose writing skills—at the time he wrote that poem—were nowhere near "honors" level. But what focus, what clarity!

Finally (ugh):

Grading/Evaluation

Let's make a few assumptions. The first is that your kids have kept a simple writing folder. (Not necessary, but helpful.) The second is that both their first and second drafts, and sometimes even third drafts, are in there. (Yes, the final drafts are in ink—a symbolic seriousness, a self-valuing; and yes, it is indeed possible that some projects, either for the individual or for the entire class, just didn't go, and are not worth the energy of a second draft; and yes, once in a while a child will write something so lovely that not a word changes from the first draft to the inky final . . .)

During your writing sessions, you've done your teacher-work: you've made the rounds, helping kids when they need help, nudging here and there, conferring deeply on occasion as the others are working, keeping your antennae receptive. You've done yourself a favor in this, for you have a good sense now of who has kept a decent level of "commitment"—as discussed earlier—and who has regarded writing time as a frivolous, quiescently anarchic lack of worksheets.

So you collect the folders not just once—as in Last Judgment—but periodically, and move toward grading.

31

You're working empirically now, looking at evidence of drafts and revisions, remembering the writing times and the student's activity or concentration during those times. You've been careful to make sure kids have been involved in a wide range of writing activities, so that a student who's simply not good at dialogue, for example, will have other areas in which to shine.

Oh, colleagues, how any one of us could write a book on the ambivalence and the inherent humanistic unfairness of our system of grading! It's hard enough to grade a spelling test, where Bennie, for instance, is progressing weekly and is now up to seven out of twenty words correct, while Mary Anne continues with her weekly twenty-out-of-twenty, and this done with her left hand, while with her right hand she's writing sheet music for the cheerleaders' song. Ben's hand is hardly finished the third word when the fourth and fifth come across him like waves, overwhelming him in the alphabetic foam and chaos . . . oh, Ben—what do I give you? An "F"? A kind "D"?

We could go on and on—all of us. We could linger on what "progress" really means, about what effect that "C" might have on a kid's feelings—yes, *feelings*—the kid who *loved* the writing sessions, put his whole self into them, and after nine weeks of hard work receives that most passionless of all grades, the circle broken and emptied, the "C."

I'm not much of a bleeding heart—having given my share of final "F's"—but I say that in the case of creative writing we do best to chicken out. To hell with the Standardized Testers. I say grade the folders with a simple plus (+) or minus (–), depending *solely upon the effort you witnessed and evident in the folder:* not on creativity, originality, or volume of writing in any given assignment. With these marks might go a short comment. ("What fine writing, Emily." "Liked reading these again, Dante." "I sure hope you try next time, Milton—I know you can do it!")

You've already commented much, both orally and in writing, on the works themselves. And certainly there are plenty of other areas within the English curriculum where we can grade in the way our schools demand. So let this writing "grade" satisfy the student's need for on-going or overall evaluation, and serve at the same time as a sense of closure for both him and for you.

* * *

Enough. Thank you for staying. On to the work!

THE WORK

The sun! The sun! And all we can
   become!
And the time ripe for running to the
   moon!
In the long fields, I leave my father's
   eye;
And shake the secrets from my deepest
   bones;
My spirit rises with the rising wind;
I'm thick with leaves and tender as a
   dove,
I take the liberties a short life permits—
I seek my own meekness;
I recover my tenderness by long looking.
By midnight I love everything alive.
Who took the darkness from the air?
I'm wet with another life.
Yea, I have gone and stayed.

                              —Theodore Roethke,
              from "What Can I Tell My Bones"[1]

CHAPTER TWO

Poetry

On Poetry

The poet is like a child awakening from slumber. He or she tries to shake off the blanket of conventional perception and reality in order to retrieve innocence and, ultimately, human possibility. The poet does so by interpreting memory in order to frame its meaning. Within the structure of language, he or she can invent almost anything—a doll, a landscape, an idea, a dream. By merely naming, the object exists. Naming is empowerment. It gives the subconscious a vocabulary of meaning, which becomes a shared vocabulary with an audience.

The creative process by which such alchemy occurs is a solitary ritual performed by a poet with his words. Every wise teacher knows that he or she may devise the means by which the student can be led to drink from the naming well, but the act of drinking itself, is the creative process—intuitive and private. Sometimes a student will reach in and emerge with a beautiful poem that he thought he was incapable of. Other times, a student who is failing in school will turn up with such an unusually fresh and unique flair for language that his teachers are prompted to look twice at the name on the poem to believe it. Poetry is the unpredictable mirror of the human mind. Once a child discovers the key, it unlocks imaginary doors.

—Genny Lim

I begin with poetry for good reason.

Poetry is little taught in our schools—either the reading of it or the writing of it. Strange: for of all genres, its the easiest with which to work.

Almost anything can be poetry. Strange newspaper articles broken into lines, snatches of overheard conversation broken into call-and-response stanzas, nonsense words, weird words repeated over and over, sentences too strange for everyday prose, prayers, meditations . . . the list is nearly infinite.

Yet sometimes we teachers have a perception that poetry is *sophisticated, intellectual,* and that we can only do justice to poetry after we've successfully run the obstacle course of reading "good literature" and writing "good prose." And reading more good literature, and writing more good prose. "I'll just get the kids through this grammar book and have them do one more essay—*then* we'll have time to get to poetry." Something like that.

The motivation on the teacher's part? I'm not sure. In some cases, I think it's anger against the bad, deadly boring work we often were taught as kids; who'd want to send kids suffering through that hell again? In other cases, I think that keeping the writing and reading of poetry "until the end" (an end often unattained) is the result of a teacher's deep love of poetry—a desire to teach it right and justly, or not at all.

Other times, we think of poetry as something rarefied and distant. The writer Bill Edmondson took his son to one of those World Wrestling Federation matches recently. You're probably familiar with the kind: fake wrestlers with names like The Hulk, The Destroyer, and Frenchy the Crusher. The villains make outrageous speeches to incite the hatred of the drunken crowd; opponents throw each other around the mat, rant, rave, and toss each other again until, in the end, good or evil emerges victorious. Rematch! Rematch!

Edmondson writes of this particular night:

> *It figures that anyone named The Genius had to be a villain, and long before we saw the wrestler come out of the northwest tunnel, we could hear the crowd over there start in on him. Their roar of hatred was localized at first, then spread quickly around the jammed Oakland Coliseum and we could follow his advance toward the ring by the bulge of fans rising and rippling forward. We still couldn't see him, only a flash of turquoise now and then through the light-blue of police shirts surrounding, and if you've ever seen a gopher burrow along*

under a lawn, his progress was kind of
like that.

Then he got to the ring and
started to climb in, and we saw that the
sparkling turquoise was the cap and
gown of a graduate. When the full crowd
saw that, it set off another wave of
sound: catcalls, and a small shower of
wadded beer cups.

At ring center, he reached up and
grabbed the suspended microphone. He
had brown hair curling to his shoulders
and a short brown mustache and beard.

"You . . . White . . . Trash . . ." he
began, and, when he had everybody's attention, "You do not deserve to have the
World's Smartest Man—which I am—en-
tertain you." By now, hundreds of
children were standing on seats to see
above their parents, who also stood
mocking, shaking their fists toward the
Genius who now moved around the ring.

He moved the way they all knew
the educated must move, little schoolyard skips, awkward and out-of-scale,
then he paused to let the gown slip
gently from his huge shoulders, and in a
final, fastidious touch, folded the robe
neatly, smoothing any tiny wrinkles,
took off the mortarboard, made a neat

pile of the vestments, and handed it down outside the ring.

Now the fans were primed for their avenger, the hero, to enter and do what they couldn't: kick this guy's pansy ass!

But The Genius wasn't quite finished taunting them. Grabbing the mike again and turning a slow circle, he unrolled a small scroll he'd traded for the cap and gown. They knew it; now he was going to say that most hated of all words, say it right to their faces, and they rose and raised their arms to fend it off.

"All right, you scum," he yelled, and there was no escape. "Now, I'm going to read you . . .

"a POEM!"[1]

So: the popularization of poetry. Think of it! Is this what poetry has become in our society? Perceived as a pursuit of pseudointellectuals, or even of intellectuals? No wonder teachers don't want to teach it and kids turn up their noses at it! It's for the elite.

But it's not for the elite. To the contrary. As a teacher, I say that poetry is an *exquisitely* good way to *open* the world of writing to kids. And the definition of *kids* here can be wide: not just gifted or mainstream students, but

---

[1] Used with permission of the author.

also students with a real aversion to writing and perhaps a real lack of writing skills.

Poetry can be *so open, so fail-safe.* Assuming you considered the discussion on rhyme in the introduction, we can move to further ground.

Eureka! Here's a medium of writing where it's all O.K.! Lines don't need to be capitalized. Punctuation can be manipulated to a student's content, and mistakes can be made to "work." Complete sentences need not be used.

Absolute sequential logic need not be followed— "leaps" are indeed encouraged! Poetry can be short or long, wild or contained, cold or passionate, consistent or varying . . . it's all O.K.!

As poet and playwright Genny Lim says in introducing this section, "Once a child discovers the key, that key unlocks imaginary doors." It's curious Genny didn't say *doors of the imagination* but, instead, *imaginary doors.* How perfect, how true, and what a wonderful way to move toward a fluency in *any* form of writing—a fluency that comes from within the student himself.

These things, coupled with the idea that *giving kids the notion that they can write poetry, their poetry, is a gift to last a lifetime,* makes me wonder why more teachers don't begin with the poem and move toward the wider fields of prose as the year progresses.

Who among us has never written a poem? Very few. These activities will get the words rolling as a student moves toward his or her Declaration of Poetic Independence.

Dictionary Poem

Dictionary poems are old stand-by poetry activities which seem always to work. They're used to get kids who are "stuck" writing, to introduce poetry writing, or to enhance kids' ability to make "bridges" or "synapses" between words.

Start small: perhaps with five or six words. Have the kids run their fingers through a dictionary and pick out *accessible* words. Write those five or six words on the board.

Now tell the kids, "It's your job to make a poem using these words. The rule is: one of the special words to a line. You can put the words in any order—just make sure that when your poem's finished, you have five lines and have used all five words. If you want to use the same word twice, that's fine."

They'll get into it, and you'll often get some fine poems from this. There are many good variations of this activity, and, if you're intending to try the Dictionary Poem, you may find other variations you prefer.

Variation #1: Dictionary Poem

Have one particular student pick all of the words.

Variation #2: Dictionary Poem

Teacher chooses the words.

Variation #3: Dictionary Poem

Use only nouns, or verbs, or adverbs, or adjectives. This does bind the imaginations of some kids, however.

Variation #4: Dictionary Poem

Use fourteen words, and teach the concept of *sonnet*.

Variation #5: Dictionary Poem

Use words of only one syllable, and stipulate that no words in the poem may be of more than one syllable.

Variation #6: Dictionary Poem

For advanced classes, use only polysyllabic words, and stipulate that no word in the poem may be of fewer than two syllables. Use your own judgment as to whether to exempt articles and conjunctions.

Variation #7: Dictionary Poem

A dictionary poem without the dictionary: Kids call out the words using their own intrinsic vocabulary.

Variation #8: Dictionary Poem

A dictionary poem without the poem: List many words on the board and tell the kids to include them in a quick *story*. (Not a very exciting activity, but collaborative group work heightens its enjoyment.)

Poem
(Dictionary)

The appetite of oneself is
somewhat like a Chihuahua.
But then again, oneself can also
darken like a galaxy without stars.
Your mind can also wander around
like a moon galloping through
daring places.
While your conscience lashes you
to a larder to keep your appetite
increasing.
Yourself can be like a lasso
roaming around in big circles.
Eat good things, and you will
dazzle like a shooting star
racing through the midnight air.

—Suzanne Healey

Name Poems:
Meditation on a Name

There are many different kinds of "name poems," but we'll just offer two here.

The first one is the meditation-type poem.

Ask the kids to close their eyes and think of *one* of their names. It might be their first name, middle, or last.

Now, use guided imagery or suggestion to get them to really meditate on their name! How does it feel? What does it look like? Does it have a certain scent? What is it doing? Moving? Where? What images (pictures) come to mind when you see your name, or when someone says your name, or when you now think of your name? Is your name like a place?

Have the kids write about it in poetry, not worrying about how many lines, or rhyme, etc. Let their imaginations go.

Variation: Name/Initial Poem

Kids like this. Have them spell their name vertically down the page. You might suggest using only the *first* name initially and then, if the student wants to, progress to other names.

The student then writes a poem using these letters as first letters of lines. The poem should be a meditation on herself, and should talk about herself.

I'm not crazy about the form of this activity which lets kids grab random words that might or might not describe themselves, such as:

Muscular, mighty
Independent, irresistible
Krafty
Educated and energetic

How dead and utterly nondescriptive! Try instead insisting that kids use the letters as starting points to cohesive lines about themselves, perhaps like:

Muscular and able to climb
Invincibly up the tree, I grab
Kernels of corn from the squirrel,
Eat them, and fly away.

That type seems to have more energy (see example).

Variation #1: Initial Poem

In this, all words of the line start with the same letter and segue into the next line: "My mother moves/invisibly in Iceland/ etc. Again, the line's letters spell a name.

Variation #2: Initial Poem

There must be a name for this form, but I don't know it. Here, a student's first name forms the vertical beginning of the lines, and the last name forms the end letters of the lines.

48

It really helps to have symmetrical names here. However, names, of course, need not be used. Messages (propagandistic, love, cryptic) can be used as well.

Start small. This is a tough activity to pull off, and takes great student concentration. Not recommended for kids with a low frustration threshold, but highly recommended for those who can plug away for the joy of creating this.

Like this:

L	A
O	L
V	W
E	A
R	Y
S	S

. . . and the kids fill in the words, making sure they fit the beginnings and endings. Try it yourself! (You can see I chickened out on the last page . . .)

Final note: Don't be tyrannical about having the *last* letters line up justified in a row. Let them have uneven margins. It's *very* difficult to choose precise enough words to line up both sides. Kudos to the kid who can do it!

Variation #3: Initial Poem

In this variation, instead of using your own name, another name is used. A friend? An enemy? (Watch out for this—sometimes not a good idea.) Your mother?

Once loose, kids will want to do a few of these.

Variation #4: Initial Poem

This is the same kind of poem (initials at the beginning of each line), but the poem is longer and spells out a message. For example, "Did you go to the show last night?" would be a poem of eight stanzas, and twenty-six lines long.

It is super if kids can not only compose a message, but also write the poem on the theme held inside the message. Subject matter for the above example might be movies, the message-receiver's relationship with her companion at the show, the message-sender's feelings of lineliness at not having been allowed to leave the house, on and on.

This activity is more fun if kids can exchange papers and act on those papers they receive, perhaps writing return poetry-messages. Legal note passing!

Name Poem

Cynthia's my name, boys are my game.

Yellow is the color of a sunny day, when
all the boys come out to play.

Not being shy will help,

To tell him just how you felt.

Heck—if that doesn't work then,

I say to try again

All the things above are true, some will
even make you blue.

Brown is a common name.

Round and round the world again.

Over, under, in a tree,

Where could an uncommon name be?

Nowhere—so I'll let my name free.

—**Cynthia Brown**

Self-Portrait in Similes

Genny Lim does this activity very successfully. I've seen its results, and love it.

At pains to teach the concept of *simile* or *metaphor*? Fear not—this poetry activity comes to the rescue.

Kids are asked to focus their thinking specifically on their face and head. The idea of *simile* is introduced or repeated. Examples are given, using *like* or *as*.

Now, the students are asked to "paint" a portrait of themselves, using similes. "My chin is like an upside-down mountain. My cheeks are like smooth dark lakes." And so on (see example).

As always, encourage kids to exhaust the possibilities for images. Have they covered every part of their head and of their face? (Keep going!) Lines can be cut later if students are not happy with them.

For me, *metaphors* seem the next logical step.

How to do it? Simply ask the kids to take their finished simile poems and chop out the "like" or "as" of each line. Magic! Instant metaphors—more immediate than similes, and often strong enough to bring a smile to the well-described mouth of each student!

Self-Portrait

My hair is like carpet that's just been
   vacuumed.
My eyes are like acorns simmering in
   warm milk.
My eyelashes are like long threads
   stitched together.
My eyebrows are like peach-fuzz, soft
   and smooth.
My cheeks are flat, as if they had been
   smashed by rocks.
My mouth is the tunnel of love.
My lips stay sealed, usually, but they are
   like soft pillows filled with water.
My tongue is like a wet sponge, but very
   soft.

—**Vaughn Davis**

Perversions of Similes

Get a list of trite similes for the kids. Better yet, elicit some from the kids. Similes like these are what we're looking for: *wise as an owl, proud as a peacock, red as a beet, slow as a turtle, sly as a fox, strong as an ox, light as a feather, sharp as a tack, flat as a pancake, smooth as silk,* ad nauseum.

Have the kids take these similes and change the endings: "Flat as a possum squashed on the road" might be one.

After the kids have gone down the list, ask them to write a poem using the similes in alternate lines. The beginning of a poem might go like this:

> *Flat as a possum squashed on the road*
> *I slipped through the crack in your*
> *door.*
> *Light as helium from the popped*
> *balloon,*
> *my hand touched your cheek in the*
> *night.*

and on, until the student is satisfied with the poem.

Sounds I Love/Sounds I Hate

Kids are much more aware of sounds than adults are.

This activity is best done meditatively at first, it seems. I turn the lights off (there *are* windows in our class, thank goodness) and ask the kids to put their heads down.

Then the teacher begins a low, gentle-voiced explanation, something like this:

> *All of us in our childhood think of certain kinds of sounds around our houses, and how those sounds make us feel. Our dog barking in the middle of the night might scare us. The sound of a mother's footsteps passing our bedroom as she goes to bed might comfort us. We might hate the sound of dishes going into the sink, because we know we have to wash those dishes. We might love the sound of a parent coming in the front door, and the rustle of grocery bags. Or, just outside our window, we might love or hate the sound of the garbage men coming in the morning.*
>
> *Think of the sounds you love around your house. Think of the sounds you really hate. And when you're ready,*

> put your head up, and on your paper
> tell us about those sounds Maybe start
> with the ones you love, and go to the
> ones you hate.

Or some introduction like that. This activity is good because it not only gets kids to focus on those details, but, in a second draft, can move from *telling* to *showing*, from:

> I hate the sound of my father putting ice
>   into his glass as he gets more
>   bourbon . . .
> (factual, prosy)

to:

> the plink, plink of ice in the glass —
> more bourbon, more bourbon . . .

This one can yield some good writing. What began as a simple "list" can end, still a kind of "list," as an evocative poem.

Chant Poem

Have the kids individually think of the beginning of a line they like and might like to repeat. Draw some examples on the board:

> The wild horse .
> The woman of the night . .
> My blood boils
> Running from you

Use these if you need to, but you'll be able to come up with better ones of your own.

Now tell the kids to write a poem using their personal chant line. They simply start with the line, then finish it, then do it again.

Try to situate things so that the feeling of *passion* envelops the room. Let the chant be a *strong* one when you demonstrate it.

Let the kids work for a while. Encourage them to fill the page, two pages, then three pages.

Now, when most of the class comes to a stasis, tell the kids to stop, and, all together, read the work out loud. The noise will be horrible, but will light fires under them.

The next step is to have the kids read their own work to themselves, whispering it, vocalizing it. After this is done, instruct them to cross out lines that don't "work"— that sound clunky, or not in good rhythm, or not true.

Give the kids a few minutes to add lines, subtract lines, or work on the piece.

If it seems appropriate, do some peer correction

Kids *love* to read the results of this activity to the class! Schedule time for that to happen; you'll be sure to hear and see some wonderful, very strong work.

Chant Poem Variation #1: "I am . . ."

Students begin each line with "I am." Try to elicit direct comparisons. "I am a tribe that goes south, I am a ferocious fish that has no companion . . ."

Then, for the last two lines, substitute another chant, such as "You see," or "Now watch . . ." A resolution!

Chant Poem Variation #2: "We are . . ."

Same as described above. In all of these, make the attempt not to tie down students to a particular chant. Some can't handle, "I am," for instance, and should be offered a choice that ranges somewhat.

Chant Poem Variation #3, #4, #5, #6, etc.

All of the following chants bring good results You'll be able to discover some of your own as well

The girl . .
Peace is . . .
Death is . . .
It's not my fault .
Leave me alone when .
Freedom is . . .
Do what you want . .
I want to go . . .
Where is . . .
Who will . . .
When can I . . .
The lion sees . .
My people . . .
I dreamed that . .

But please: promise not to do *"Love is . . ."!*

Untitled

The woman of the night
The woman working hard
The woman with all the brains
The woman of all abilities
The woman with all heart
The woman with spirit
The woman getting paid
The woman rejoicing
The woman who works miracles
The woman always traveling
The woman supporting the poor
The woman who helps the bleeding
The woman teaching children
The woman of the world
The woman telling stories
The woman protecting people of the
    street
The woman of the night

                 —Jackie Selinger

Free at Last

At first I was in jail
Now I'm free
At first I got beat up
Now I'm free
At first I had to work for white people
Now I'm free
At first I had to peel potatoes
Now I'm free
At first I had to sit in the back of the bus
Now I'm free
At first I had to go to school
way out in the country
Now I'm free
But I was walking on the sidewalk
and the white person
went way in the other side
of the street
and I was on the sidewalk
by myself

—**Laura Pratt**

Snowball Poem (Rhopalisms)

This is a poem that accumulates words like a snowball: line one is one word, line two is two words, three is three, etc., until the poem is complete. Kids like this-it mixes puzzle with poetry.

Snowball Poem: Variation #1

A little more complicated than the first rhopalism, this variation demands that the student have only one *syllable* more in each succeeding line. This makes word choice a little more challenging.

One way to approach both of these poems is for a student to write a poem—any poem—then change words in the poem to fit the demands of the snowball rhopalism.

Snowball Poem: Variation #2

In this variation, each *stanza* is one *line* longer than the previous one.

Snowball Poem: Variation #3

Let the kids begin anew each line, making a chant if they so desire. Example: I am not lost . . . , extended, and the first few words repeated (see example).

Snowball Poem:
"I Do Not Care"

I do not care about rotten,

noisome toenails.

I do not care about gentle,

amiable, pleasing creatures.

I do not care about buying

useless, oncoming particles Brazilian

Kindhearted.

I do not care about smelly animals

silently urinating underwater.

I do not care about myself writing

snowball composite.

—**Lisa Ho**

Indefinite Pronoun Poem

The concept of indefinite pronouns can be tough to teach. This activity makes it easier.

In this activity, either give the kids a list of indefinite pronouns, or elicit such a list from the kids.

Now, assign the task: the kids are to take this list of indefinites and make a poem out of them. Say nothing more. If the kids ask whether the poem has to rhyme, say no. In fact, no rhyme is allowed! If the kids ask whether the words can be put together to form a story, simply say, "Do what you need to do in order to put these words together in a form that means something to you."

Obviously, they'll need to add other words in their work—but encourage them not to get too wordy, thus avoiding the nice effect this piece of writing can have.

Who Is Who
?

Somebody is a thief.
Anybody knows it.
Everybody tried to find out who it is, but
Nobody found it.
Nobody called the police.
Somebody got caught.
Somebody blamed it on Everybody.
Everybody said, "Anybody could have
    done it."

The police couldn't do anthing about it.
They didn't have anything to prove that
Somebody is a thief.
As everybody said before, "Anyone or
    Something
Could be the mastermind of everything."
So, Everyone was happy because nothing
Happened.

—**Luong Thai**

Arbitrary Juxtaposition Poem

You can change the form of this one any way you wish.

What works is to make a simple list on the chalkboard. For example,

> Day of the week
> City
> Animal
> Flower
> Season
> Flavor of ice cream
> Precious stone

Ask the kids to write that list—or the one you devise of similar length—on a piece of scratch paper.

Now, the task is to ask the kids individually to commit themselves to choosing one of each of these things (say, Monday, Chicago, balloon, marigold, etc.). Have them write their choices on that same paper.

Finished? Make a poem using these things in any order, doing anything, making sense or not making sense.

The idea is that, perhaps, what the kids choose are favorites of theirs, and important words to *that* student will be woven into a poem both personal and powerful.

66

Untitled

I saw a black panther
on Friday in Daly City
At first I thought it was
a diamond—he was waving
in the white roses. It
seemed very strange to me, 'cause
it was a winter like spring
and an orange sherbet day
So I end this poem with
a silver goodbye.

—Joey Wilson

"Everyone Is Against Me" Poem

Appeal to the paranoia in kids and get them to write this "chant" poem, which lists every single place where the world conspires against them.

The poem can begin every stanza with just that line:

Everyone is against me.

Then continue with the listing—

my mother makes me clean my room every day
and my dog's fleas jump onto me.

They can end the stanza with a repetition of the "everyone is against me" theme, or just begin the next stanza with those words. Or they don't have to restate the theme at all once it's said; they can simply write the poem itemizing the tough times they have in the worlds of adults or kids.

Try it!

Everyone Is Against Me

Everyone is against me:
    my teachers give me too much
    homework, five hours a night
Everyone is against me!
Everyone is against me:
    I can't do fun things with my friends.
    My mom makes me do homework
    before I go to the wharf.
Everyone is against me!
Everyone is against me:
    I can't go the places I want to go.
    My mom likes different things than I
    do.
Everyone is against me!
Everyone is against me:
    people don't like my ideas.
    I think our school should be painted
    black and white, but other people
    don't.
Why is everyone against me?

—Osha Ashworth

Pass-It-Around Poem

This is a wonderful activity for helping kids learn—and reminding *ourselves* as teachers—that poetry needn't always make "sense" line-to-line as prose does. It lets kids know that there can be "leaps"—crazy and beautiful, like leaps of thought, like synapses in the brain—between ideas and images, and that without surprises, a poem is pretty boring. The pass-it-around poem can be done very simply and quickly—as an exercise that generates a lot of joy and laughter and then is over—or it can be extended into activities that get pretty close to the nature of poetry itself. So please do look at the variations/extensions of this work—they can be very rewarding for you and the kids.

The basic activity goes like this: each student takes out a piece of paper, and on that paper writes a single line of poetry. Encourage the kids to use their senses, to remember that lines in poetry can be phrases and don't have to be complete sentences, that lines in poetry may be questions, and so on. Any line the student writes is acceptable—there are no "rights" or "wrongs." ("Surprise us! Make the reader 'ooh' and 'aww'!")

Now the passing part begins. But before one student passes it to the student behind or in front, he or she folds the paper so that the next student can't see the line already written. The second student writes a line, folds the paper again, and passes it on. If you have a classroom whose arrangement is in rows, it's more effective to have kids pass the papers snakelike; down one row, up the next, and so on, with the very last kid rushing her paper over to the first kid on the other side of the room.

Since every kid has begun at the same time, when you say, "Change!" there should be as many papers changing hands as there are students in your class. Increase the time a bit as you go along.

Do this change a dozen or so times. Now, have the kids unfold the papers and read them. They'll love the results. Some are crazy, some hold together quite sensibly, and others, if nonsensical, may strongly convey a mood.

So: each student now holds a piece of paper. It's accordion-like, having been folded a dozen times. That paper becomes her or his particular project. The task: eliminate as many lines as he or she wishes that just don't seem to fit at all with the rest of the lines; fix verb tense or other grammar problems when they're clearly a *problem;* rearrange the order of the lines in any way desired and make a new, spectacular (if still crazy) poem out of those remaining lines. The resulting work should be at least four lines long—preferably longer—and should be given a title by the new proprietor!

You might want to talk about surrealism here, or you might not.

The example that follows ("The Traveler") is an extraordinary one. Done by a seventh-grade gifted class, it is written verbatim in the order students wrote the lines. Verb tense was changed in some of the lines to keep the poem in the present, and two lines were eliminated: *Dr. Doolittle doodles with his dinky-twinky pet* and *Boys scamper excitedly to see a fight.* Most poems won't turn out so strangely moving unless many more lines are cut and those that remain are rearranged. This seemed a rare beauty

Variation #1: Pass-It-Around Poem

Simple: either before or after doing the preceding activity, ask kids to pick out one or two lines from their paper that they like best. One by one, quickly, ask the kids to read those wonderful lines out loud. Pause to talk about a few if you like, or simply use the round robin as an infusion of energy into the rewriting process or as an *entrée* into the next variation.

Variation #2: Pass-It-Around Poem

Have kids either at home or at school take their twelve-lined papers, all of which contain hastily written and often scribbled lines, and rewrite those lines legibly. Make sure they allow for large blank spaces between the lines written.

Now, pass our scissors. Have kids cut their lines into twelve separate strips. Explain that each student will be using masking tape to tape six lines onto the chalkboard, and that they should make two piles: one pile of six lines that they think would go well in a poem, and another pile of six that they'll probably not tape up.

Circulate in the room while the kids are working on this; pass out pieces of masking tape for the taping process. Have ready a second assignment, possibly a grammar exercise, so that when taping time comes for some kids the rest are still busy. Now, have six kids or so at a time go to the sides and front of the room and tape their lines diagonally so that students walking by will easily be able to read those lines. Continue until all the class has done this. You'll have a room full of lines of poetry!

Now, as you might expect, you'll tell kids their task: in an orderly way, six or eight at a time, to "browse" among the lines of poetry and pick six that move them or attract them in some way.

Demonstrate for them. Be an actor. Walk a bit, find a line you like, read it aloud, grab it from the wall. Walk more, find another line that might go with the first, grab it. They'll get the idea. Once all the kids in the class have their six lines and are seated, give them their assignment: "Make a poem of at least four lines from the six you have chosen. Rearrange lines any way you want to. Change a few words if you need to—but only if you need to. You may need to change verb tense here and there, or change a plural to singular, and so forth. That's O.K.! Or you may be desperate to write another line to make the poem complete. Write it! You know what to do!"

While the kids are working, you pass the waste basket and quietly collect the discarded six or so lines on each desk.

Flexibility is good here. If a kid wants to keep an extra line or make a poem of three lines that seem to fit together perfectly, let it happen. Let them know that they're in control of their poems.

After the poems have been written and titled, begin reading. Here is where you can teach about poetry—about surprises, about mood, about theme, about the pure beauty of certain words beside each other—about the whole range, really. Words are malleable! Phrases and sentences are not holy, but are made to be formed and reformed!

A potent sample of this variation:

What is the answer to life?
Children laugh in the swimming pool.
In the eye of an eagle the boy is dead.
Fire spread everywhere.

Variation #3: Pass-It-Around Poem

Do the original activity, but have kids keep the first (folded) papers, and then do Variations #2 and #3.

Variation #4: Pass-It-Around Poem

After the activity, while the kids still have the accordion-like paper with many different lines on it, ask them to pick one or two lines that would make great first lines to a short story or a novel. If there still is any energy left in the activity (you'll feel it in the room), ask the kids to take one of their "great first line" choices and, for home-work, write a short story using that particular line as the first. Here are some lines I've encountered that seem like they'd be wonderful first lines; you may want to read a few of these as examples:

- *Memories come and go, but a few stick in place.*
- *I will live long, but my heart is broken.*
- *In the still of the night the black cat stroked his mighty claws against the howling wind.*
- *"Do you ever wonder about the universe?" I asked him.*

74

- The smell of roses makes me sick.
- The girl had already eaten lunch.
- I hate people who hate people for no reason.
- I drank the cool liquid but did not swallow.
- The rabbits in the forest clustered together.
- The shark grins as he approaches the submarine.
- The nerd lives in a secluded locker.
- As I run I hear my friend screaming.
- I start to feel the tears coming down.
- So how come this happened?
- I always have ideas—I just don't show 'em.
- So isn't it true that if you read this question you will activate the ancient curse?

The Traveler

The trees sway in the dead of night.
People weep around the coffin.
He sings softly in the warm spring air.
He stinks, he smells like rotting cheese
Babies' voices are like a song.
Life has no real answer.
I hear my friend scream as I shut the
    door,
Break it.
The breeze is blowing on my face.
Do I have an answer to my life?
                —**Students, Room 226,**
                Marina Middle School

The Natural Attraction

College-level writing workshops caution against anthropomorphization—giving human characteristics to nonhuman things.

Let kids learn that in college. At this age, they like to do it anyway, and who knows—it might be that human empathy exhibited in adulthood might well have as a precursor the ability to anthropomorphize freely as kids!

Enough—here's the activity.

The teacher goes to the board and asks kids to name a *few* things that naturally go together. They may come up with something like this:

> pencil & paper
> peanut butter & jelly
> table & chair

Jot down just enough to get the idea across. Don't exclude kids who might say, "kids & skateboards" or some such.

Now the teacher talks about love: how, in a love relationship, lovers first are not lovers but perhaps see each other from afar. Then, for one reason or another, get closer, then closer, then love blossoms, again in one form or another.

Have the kids write a poem about a relationship between *their own* choice of "things that go together" and how that relationship builds.

Let the kids use any kind of voice they wish: from one of the couple's point of view, from both, or from that of an omniscient observer. I complicate things by stipulating that no rhyme may be used, and that the lines ought to contain the natural breath units found in everyday speech patterns, something like this:

> *I, table, had*
> *an emptiness*
> *under me.*
> *But across the room*
> *I saw her: the chair!*
> *(etc.)*

Try it! Adventurous groups of kids love this, and you'll be surprised not only by the things that go together, but by the crazy relationships these "things" can have!

Needle and Thread

I'm just an ordinary needle
Living an ordinary life
Sewing this and stitching that
Like holes, rips, and such
But through all those years
Never have I liked the thread I used
But there came a day
When a new thread caught my eye
She was a Material Girl
Sleek and smooth
Sturdy and strong
The best strand I'd seen in days
We stared for a while
I ran to her
She ran to me
We tied the knot
And sewed all night
Needle and thread were made to be.

—Patrick Woo

Group Poem: Personification (Anthropomorphization)

These are big words (teachable!) for a simple process that's fun done in whole-class groups.

It seems best to start simple, and with abstract words that are important to us: *death, peace, grief, life, joy, sadness, wealth, hunger,* etc.

Put these words to one side of the chalkboard. Now get the students in a group to think of a person or living animal that might embody these ideas.

O.K. So some student says, "Death is a vicious dog." You extend it by saying, "Tell me more—describe it—tell me maybe what the dog is doing." The kids will extend it to, perhaps, "Death is a vicious dog with foam coming out of its mouth."

My favorite so far is: *Wealth is a polar bear riding in a limousine.*

Go down the list, hitting all of the words on the board. Voilà! You've got a good group poem the kids will take joy in.

Homework? Have the kids write down the same words and do their *own* personifications. This will work well with some classes, and not with others. You know your kids.

Some helpful word-examples: *death, peace, grief, life, joy, sadness, wealth, hunger, truth, sickness, despair,* popularity, prejudice, hope, boredom, hate, optimism, intelligence, homelessness, rage, excitement, anticipation, toxicity, innocence, poverty, exhaustion, success, helplessness, dread, satisfaction, worry, eagerness, inflexibility, ignorance, insanity, efficiency, deviousness, industriousness, laziness, luxury, dejection, enthusiasm, jealousy, piety, evil, hypocrisy, justice and injustice, honesty and dishonesty, patience and impatience . . . and add your own.

Variation: Anthropomorphization Poem

Students can take one of these qualities and make a chant-poem of it, using the same guidelines as in the group poem. What you'll have, then, is something like:

> Prejudice is . . .
> Prejudice is . . .
> Prejudice is . . . and so on.

This can make for a very powerful poem.

Lust Personified:
The Seven Deadly Sins

Well, not just lust, but that *did* get your attention. And not just the seven deadly sins, either, as comic and rigorous an exercise as it is to even bring those seven medieval monsters to mind.

This activity is somewhat like the group poem/anthropomorphization work, except: (1) it personifies or brings to life only attributes that have had heavy moral or societal judgments laid on them, and (2) the poems are written individually.

The Seven Deadlies are pride, envy, anger, sloth, avarice, gluttony, and lust. A writer could go further, certainly, moving into more tawdry or taboo realms. Murder, suicide, and incest, though clearly not parallel with the Seven Deadlies, are always contemporary topics that students often write about with deep interest and enthusiasm. Use your judgment, but before shying away from an attempt at this activity, do see high-schooler Erica Levison's stellar example of this form of writing.

Variation: Personification Poem

Of course, you don't *have* to use those unpleasant-though-real words above. In this variation, kids *individually* can take abstract words such as those mentioned in the group poem, and make these abstractions concrete by personifying them in poetry.

Again, a few random examples might be: *death, peace, grief, life, joy, sadness, wealth, hunger, truth, sickness, despair, popularity, prejudice, hope, boredom, hate, optimism, intelligence, homelessness, rage, excitement, anticipation, toxicity, innocence, poverty, exhaustion, success, helplessness, dread, satisfaction, worry, eagerness, inflexibility, ignorance, insanity, efficiency, deviousness, industriousness, laziness, luxury, dejection, enthusiasm, jealousy, piety, evil, hypocrisy, justice and injustice, honesty and dishonesty, patience and impatience,* on and on. (Great way to sneak in some vocabulary work.)

Lust

Can you see Lust over there,
falling out of her dress?
She's such a tease.
Lust has something up her sleeve.
She's got a jealous streak.
Lust has a hopeful face
with lots of lipstick painted on.
She's not very bright,
and she's frequently getting herself into
    trouble.
The other girls
like Intelligence and Self-Control
laugh at Lust.
"She's weak," they whisper from their
    quiet corner.

Lust has a younger brother named Love.
Sometimes they're seen walking around
together,
sometimes they're not.
But Lust has a bad sense of direction,
and her brother is very calm and wise.
She's less scared of what she's capable of
when he's with her.

—Erica Levison

Graffiti Poem

Get the kids individually to start to notice and write down bits of graffiti they see—in the bathroom, on a downtown wall, on the seat of a bus, and so on.

Do what you can to encourage a good collection of graffiti.

When the assemblages are bulging, ask the kids to arrange their bits of graffiti into poems. These poems may or may not contain their own thoughts or graffiti, the graffiti may or may not be interspersed with comments . . . in short, let the kids be the experimenters with this poem, and enjoy the results, both rhythmically and aesthetically!

Graffiti

Sex-drugs and Rock-N-Roll
Another style is the one called soul.
Welfare day is 1st and 15th
Be on time to the foodstamp line
People write on walls and don't know
What it means.
When they get busted and go to jail
They momma come with the broom
Go back to El Salvador they say.
But little do they know, this world
Belongs to everyone.

You see what graffiti can do.
It doesn't do anything. Not for you
All it does is waste your ink—
You destroy the property
And think someone will like it.
Keep walls clean unless they're yours
Don't waste your time just stay cool,
    calm, innocent
                —Darlene Mulitauaopele

Concrete Poetry

Poems are so often so linear!

Concrete poems break those lines. They still use words, but tell kids *change me!* Form me like clay! Let kids make words, or words put together, or long poetic lines of words flowing and flowing, in a new way.

A poem about an apple can look like an apple. Poems about rain can be vertical, no? Wouldn't a poem about a new car look great formed in the shape of a car?

Similarly, single words can be concrete poems. Pig can be drawn to look like a pig, can't it?

Unlimited possibilities exist here. Let the kids go on this one.

Go to the Word-Well!

Most kids have no idea what a *well* really is, but have seen cartoon re-creations of the brick well: the bucket on the pulley, the water dripping from the sides of the bucket . . .

This concept can be used to facilitate poetry writing, too! Indeed, don't we all go into our own "word-wells" when we speak or write?

Go the chalkboard and draw a *large* image of the outline of a well. Don't draw bricks—just the outline.

Now, ask the kids to start calling out words to you. Write quickly, get the words to come quickly, and fill the well with words—words sideways, words vertically, words horizontally and diagonally. Write as many words as you can.

Now the kids themselves write a poem. They are to use words in the well when they need to go "fishing." You might suggest they begin each line with one of the "well-words." Encourage the use of other words as well (forgive me), and let this be an exercise that flows freely as water—no other guidelines.

Upside-Down Poem

Tell the kids, "Pretend you are a person who lives his life upside down. Somehow, you walk on your hands and see the whole world upside down. Write a poem telling about how you feel being like this, telling about what things look like from an upside-down point of view, and how you feel about life like this."

Encourage actual descriptions of objects from an upside-down point of view.

This poem might inspire some kinetic activity; plan for that if it's desirable.

This activity can as well be translated to prose, but perhaps would lack the extra "bite" of a well-written poem.

Other-Perspective Poems

This activity, too, can be translated to prose, and perhaps more readily than the upside-down poem.

Have the kids imagine that they have a perspective they cannot possibly have: that of an eagle in the sky, that of an ant, that of the moon looking at earth, a head louse in a forest of hair, variations nearly infinite.

Have the kids write from that perspective a poem that includes *lots* of description. What does it look like? Other senses should be integrated as well.

Perspective Poem Extension

Now have the kids write a poem (or piece of prose) from the *other* point of view: earth speaking to and of the moon, the head describing the louse, whatever seems opposite and appropriate.

Life Upside Down

Life upside down is different from life
right side up.
I walk on the sky.
I look up at the ground.
I feel sick when I see people running —
I begin to get oh so dizzy!
Life upside down is like . . .
living your life on a rollercoaster
full of twists and turns.
When it flips—I'm right side up.
Instead of living right side up
I've realized I like my life
upside down.

—**Alison Mouser**

ſ

New Perspectives

There is a famous Wallace Stevens poem entitled "Thirteen Ways of Looking at a Blackbird." If you can get that poem, read it to the kids. They won't understand it, but that's O.K. It offers thirteen short stanzas whose language is beautiful; each stanza is indeed a new perspective.

Have the kids pick and meditate on a person or an object. Now, ask the kids to write from as many *perspectives* as they can.

Let's choose, say, a woman sleeping. The different perspectives written from might be: of the flea at the bottom of her foot, of her lover half-awake with one eye open, of the spider on the ceiling, of the alarm clock at her bedside table, of the picture of her son on the bureau facing her, of the mirror on her table, of the dream she now is having, on forever!

Have the kids write short poems in such different perspectives. This is the *physical* world we're talking about here, of course; some kids, being more cerebral, will want to write on many different *mental* perspectives, and good for them!

Perspective: Classroom

The teacher stares out
into a sea of young faces.
He remembers—
remembers when he was young.

A student listens intently.
He knows the teacher is wise.
He dreams of what the teacher was like
when he was young.

A desk feels a student
carving into it.
The desk is in pain
but cannot say a word
for it has no mouth.

A book—all tattered and torn—
is sad as it sits on a desk.
It is full of knowledge
If only someone were to care enough to
    read it.

—Heather Cloke

Eavesdropping
without a Warrant

We all overhear snatches of conversation that are just *great*—"I shan't go to that shop anymore no matter how good their hamburger is . . ." You know. If our ears are open, delight and amusement await us every day.

In this activity, kids are encouraged to open their ears.

They make a little hand-sized notebook out of any kind of paper—scrap included.

Then, during a given period of time (a week seems best, with daily reminders from the teacher at appropriate times), kids jot down overheard snatches of conversation. Anything. Words said in *anger* might be a specialty to one student. Another might choose to overhear and jot down words having to do with *romance*. A third might scribble randomly words and phrases that simply strikes her as *sounding good*—maybe just musical, maybe rhythmic, maybe strange, anything.

The job at the end? Write 'em so that they go together. This is not a dialogue, but a pastiche of human conversation. Some kids might like to hear a suggestion that their poem could sound like a crowd on a city street; others might like no suggestion at all—just a chance to artfully arrange their conversational fragments, discarding some, putting some here, some there .

A classwide reading certainly is indicated here, and, as we termed it many years ago, "expansion of consciousness" can certainly occur as a by-product of this writing activity!

Number Talk/Letter Talk

Numbers are numbers, no? They have meaning. they are the symbols we use when we count.

Letters are letters, right? Put with others, they have meaning. They help us talk. Or *is* that true? Maybe they just help us write.

These ideas in themselves are fun to talk about with groups of kids. Kids are closer than we are to the basic idea of decoding.

In this activity, though, we step back from the use of numbers or letters, and have kids concentrate and write about their *form*.

What does a *one* look like? An arrow pointed toward the sky? A thumb sticking up from underground? What message is that arrow sending? What message comes from the thumb?

Now, what does a *two* seem to represent? An electric wire coiled on the street? A wild hair?

And is the *three* the pitchfork chasing 1 and 2?

You see the drift here. The poem aims to describe numbers or letters in strictly unconventional terms.

The best way to go about this activity, it seems, is to go through a few and talk about the pictorial possibilities these numbers (or letters) have. Then, encourage students to write poems that progress through *at least ten* numbers, either speaking to the reader in the number's voice or describing the picture (and the use, perhaps) a given number evokes for them.

Some kids will get stuck on this one—victims of too much rote learning. But encourage them—one by one, so to speak. They *will* get it, and will have fun with this activity.

Number Talk

1 is a line. A line, that is all.
2 is curvey. Try not to fall!
3 is a bird. Flying up high.
4 is a flagpole. Waving goodbye.
5 is unique. It has no special shape.
6 is something you wear—a rolled-up
    cape.
This is the end of my number poem.
I hope you liked it. I have to go home!
          —Nicole Vaugn

Focus!

Ask the kids to write a poem on an object that gets all of their attention: where they really look at the object deeply—with new eyes—and talk about it. Examples? The hair of the girl in front of them, a particular flower or blade of grass (good activity to do outside), part of a cyclone fence, whatever catches their attention. The object can be given a memory, too, if the writer desires that.

Do try to direct this activity away from simple description. While it's valuable, that's not what you're looking for here. You're looking for poetry—maybe words repeated over and over, maybe associations, similes, metaphors, the feeling that the object seems to express by its presence, and other essences that are not merely attributes.

Unreal Translation

In this activity, the teacher makes photocopies of a poem in another language—the more obscure the language the better.

Now the kids are asked to "translate" the poem, line for line. Of course, they won't be able to do it (as would neither you nor I), so ask them, line for line, to make up what the poem might be saying. Emphasize that there is no right or wrong to this work—just adventure. Encourage humor, but don't demand it. You'll get some fine serious "translations" too.

This is a good time to work with the idea of *association*. Does that German word *Antwort* remind you of a wart on an ant? (Direct). Does the word *gefleckt* make you think of what someone might say to a person he's angry at? Does *pikfein Pfau* make you think of three brothers? (Very indirect). Poetry springs from such "mistakes"!

Real Translations

This activity can be done on a selected basis, perhaps as extra credit, or for self-motivated kids.

Find some *good, clear,* and not too lengthy poetry in your student's native language. Ask her or him to translate it and, with his or her permission, read the work to the class.

This can be the beginning of lessons on translation—its difficulty, how important and especially difficult it is to translate poetry, how different translators of the same poem can come up with completely different meanings, and other issues.

Shoes of Loneliness: Surrealistic Juxtapositions

Duane BigEagle introduced surrealism into my class by doing this exercise.

Kids fold a blank piece of paper in half the vertical way.

On the left side, they list vertically ten *things* of their choice (for instance: *shoes, jacket, book, pants,* television, binder, chair, Ferrari, pen, tie, dictionary, sweater, jewelry, lipstick, flower).

On the right side, kids are told to list vertically ten feelings (e.g., happiness, pain, conceitedness, jealousy, shyness, embarassment, sadness, joy, fear, gloominess, selfishness, despair, anger, tenderness).

Now, between the two, on the crease of the paper, the word *of* is written on each line.

What you've got now are ten phrases, each of which sounds something like "Shoes of Loneliness."

Now the kids write a poem, using the phrases in any order they wish.

The poem can be story-like (*In the morning I woke up to watch my TV of jealousy./I wore my pants of madness and my shirt of love/etc.*) or poetry-like (*Where did it all begin?/Did it begin with clothes of envy,/or the pen of loneliness?*).

Kids really enjoy this work, and its lack of "normal" logical sequence.

Untitled

As I walk through the country of happiness, I pick flowers of bravery. But the flowers went inside my shoes of terror. As I went on I saw a garden of joyfulness. As I looked in the garden of joyfulness I saw my boyfriend of excitedness. The picture of anxiousness is blocking my mind. Thinking about the heaven of loneliness, I thought about the god of depression. As I walk through the rabbits of ugliness, they hop on my ribbon of loveliness.

—Mayra M. De Vera

Title Tyrannies: Poetry

Usually, when teachers require that a student write on a certain title, what results is *deadly*: boring to the student and teacher alike, filled with adult expectations.

Try taking this moldy form and changing it. Make up some crazy titles, or *one* crazy title, and ask the class to write on it.

Some sample titles?

"Why I Left You"
"The Heaviness of My Foot"
"The Underwear of Books"
"Climbing a Sideways Ladder"
"To My Love in My Next Life"

You can make your own. Do. The kids need to be loose for this one, used to writing on unorthodox things. Otherwise they'll panic and freeze. A properly writing-lubricated class will respond to these titles, or any, admirably.

You choose whether to be tyrannical about just one title for the entire class, or many. Remember that in diversity there is choice.

Arcane Word Poem

Go to the school library and get the big Webster's dictionary. Pick out ten or so very strange and little-used words. Write down their etymologies and their meanings.

Bring the list to class, and put the words on the board. Tell the kids that *you* didn't know what these words meant before this morning's library research. Now tell the kids that they'll be writing a poem, using all of the words somewhere in their poem. No fair looking up the words in the dictionary! The kids have to *guess* what the words mean, and use them in that "guess form" inside the poem.

Collect the poems when you decide they should be due. Read them, noting where some kids actually come close to the meaning.

If you choose, assign particular students the task of looking up the words. Ten kids, ten words, etc.

This activity not only gets students to take chances, but also underscores the concepts of the music in words, ignorance common to us all, and scholarly research. Some fine poems come of this activity.

It should be emphasized that, though a child defines a word incorrectly in this activity, she or he is not "wrong," but brave!

Some sample words: *kloof, calque, cockatrice, discaid, ensile, pavid, recusant, stipiate, whyo, milksop.* (You'll have fun finding your own . . .)

CHAPTER THREE

Prose

B

efore we dive toward prose activities, a few things might be said.

The first is that the nature of the prose writing in this book is quite different, it is to be hoped, than that of most expository/essay work students encounter so often. The ideas depend on the self, and, again, on imagination.

Certainly the trend these days is to ask students to write from their own experience. The rationale for this concept is important, and complicated, and I won't oversimplify it here.

Kids have experience. We all do. And all of us like to communicate our experiences to others. It's human.

But I worry that insistence on *writing from experience* will be misinterpreted as a mandate to force kids to *write from direct, day-to-day experience only.* This would be a tragically mistaken notion, I think, and would do a great disservice not only to individual selves and lives, but to the future of imagination.

When I taught very young children, we began from the premise that kids of that age operate almost wholly from ego; they're masses of ego-in-motion. It's reasonable to teach from that, then.

As kids grow older (or, older, *grow*), we do them and the world a favor, I think, by assuming them not to be masses of ego but human beings who, while certainly deeply involved in concerns of self, have the capacity to move *out* of self and toward "otherness."

This is where I have problems with what I see as an overemphasis on personal experience in writing with middle-school-and-older kids.

Please don't get me wrong: I believe *certainly* that kids' experience is profound, meaningful, and insightful not just to them but to many. And I believe deeply not only in kids writing often from their own observations and experience, but in such writing serving as a "core" of a school year's body of writing work.

But some part of me becomes panicky and claustrophobic when I think of the effect *on the self and on society* of thousands and even millions of older students writing solely from personal experience and observation. How many millions of expository/autobiographical essays are assigned yearly in our schools? We could pave all the interstate highways in the nation with such papers.

And papers wherein the the student is encouraged or chooses to go out of self and into another realm of the imagination? Too few, in my view.

I may be mistaken, but it seems that only when a student can take himself or herself *out* of his or her environment and imaginarily put that self *into* another—another life, another time, another set of experiences, another place—can the seeds of *compassion* sprout and take root: for the self and for our society.

We could go on and on. You might argue that only when the self is fully explored and known is a human being capable of compassion. I'd want to challenge that.

Let's not argue, though. Let's just allow for now that the fictive possibility is important; we can agree on that.

All of this is by way of introducing this prose section, and saying, in effect, that the fictive possibility is what's important in this section: not autobiographical accuracy. Fiction certainly may be *created* from a core of experience, but this doesn't necessarily follow. Again, allowing kids latitude and room to move is paramount in these activities.

Finally, a quick word on evaluation of prose ideas found in this book.

Currently, there is a process called "holistic evaluation" being used well in schools. It began, I think, as a process of the Bay Area Writers Workshop. In it, prose work — most often expository essays — is scored on a one-to-six basis, one being the worst and six the best. Students participate in scoring, as do adults in the classroom. Criteria for each category are well understood by all, and the process, if done right, is not only nonthreatening, but extremely helpful to young prose writers.

Inspired as that process is, I feel quite uncomfortable in advocating that it be used as an evaluative tool in the activities to follow. The nature of the activities simply doesn't invite it. Really, I suppose that the activities in the following section are more *poems that have overrun their bounds* than traditional prose. As such, many of the works written will be extremely personal, and inappropriate, I think, to discuss at length and "score" as if they were *measurable* in any true way. They're not, and the private process of composing many of these works would be violated in such an arena.

However, that's not to say that many of the activities' results should not be discussed in class! Certainly many lend themselves to lots of discussion: the diaries, the group stories, fable-making, personal ad codes, phony research reports, and many others. Clearly, not only will students want to share their work here, but, since humor is the key to so many, the class as a whole will dearly want to listen.

Too, it's certainly valid to probe and ask public questions—especially in story-oriented work. This questioning is not only helpful for the writer, but also helps the class think in terms of basic questions to ask themselves as they write. But too many prewriting and postwriting activities will eviscerate the intention and immediacy of many of these activities.

I would hope that the teacher would look at this work, then, in a very different light from most prose collected during the year: it will have a life of its own, and that life will reflect the second, secret lives of your students.

Story: Group Activity

Have the kids get into groups. Maximum number is four. Five if there's a lonely straggler. Each student gets out a piece of paper. Make up a crazy first sentence to a story, "The horse, having long ago run away from home, was lonely." Each student writes that down. All the better if a student makes up the first line.

Now, with your timer on your desk, tell the kids that they have one minute to write the next sentence. Encourage humor and craziness, but don't force it. After the timer rings, have them rotate papers and write the next line on the next paper. One minute, then switch. As the story lengthens, extend time slightly.

The first time this activity is done, it should be relatively short—maybe ten sentences. Kids will naturally extend it later. Don't forget to give kids warning before you intend to end it; say something like, "O.K., only three more times are coming, so think about writing some ending sentences!"

Kids love this activity, and good ideas comes of it. Peer proofreading and second/third drafts can come next.

If students request a repetition of the "group story," be sure to have *them* choose the first line the next time around.

Variation/Extension: Group Story

Same format, except this time you warn the kids you'll be going many more times around, and therefore they'll have to *develop* characters, setting, conflict, denouement, etc. (A good chance to teach the word *denouement.*)

You can help by introducing some elements. Tell the kids that they can write almost anything they want, but that *each finished story* must have in it the following elements: an animal (any), a mystery to be solved (any), and a game (any) that figures importantly in the mystery's solution.

Kids will gripe at first about this, but *great* stories come from it, and they do indeed respond to the challenge. (And don't be tied to the elements listed above; vary them with your own, but try not to include so many that kids get overwhelmed.)

Again, the peer proofreading and second/third draft processes are appropriate next.

Why Did She Leave?

Once there was a beautiful lady. She had long, red, frizzy hair. It reached all the way down to her legs. She had cherry red lips. She was a nice lonely girl.

Every day she would pick flowers and fruits. She would go to the forest and give the animals the things that she picked. Because of her kindness, the animals in return guided her home.

She wanted to do something to repay them. So one day she went to her nearby Safeway and bought some potato chips, dips, and some fruit punch. She had also made some pastries the night before for the forest party.

At the party they had a ball. They played games and talked. Soon, the party was over. She thanked them once again.

The young lady kept visiting the forest and the forest animals every day. Then one day she didn't come. This happened for two weeks straight! So the animals one day went to visit her, but she wasn't there. She was gone!

Nobody knew what happened to her, so they always kept these questions in mind: "Is she mad at us? Why? Where is she?"

But still, nobody knows where she went. So when you're walking through the woods or forest you can hear the animals sniffing everywhere, looking for her.

—**Vivian Dominguez**
—**Adele Martinez**
—**Maureen Herrera**

Fable-Making

Aesop could do it: why not kids?

This activity is of course introduced by the reading of a few fables—whether by Aesop or someone more modern. But choose relatively simple, short ones for the first run of this activity!

Perhaps your kids have had a steady diet of fables all year. All the better, but not essential!

I like to start a little discussion by getting kids to speculate as to how Aesop might have gone about the *writing* of his fables. We've seen that they involve animals. How did he choose the animals? Is it possible he was walking in the forest, saw two animals, sat down on a rock, and began writing a story about an interaction between the two creatures?

Or, perhaps, did he first think about what lesson—or moral—he wanted to teach, then create a story around that moral?

My hunch is the second, but what difference does it make? The important thing is to get kids thinking about structuring their own fable—a plan for their action!

So, obviously, after this introduction, the teacher has the kids write their own fables. Usually, they involve animals and the illustration of a moral. That should be encouraged; however, if someone comes up with a more modern fable replacing animals with, say, animate kitchen appliances, bravo!

Variation: Fables

Kids love to complain about the unfairness of their parents, or about how their parents never pay any attention to their opinions.

Have the kids think of a lesson they'd like to communicate to their parents. It might be about fairness, listening to their children's wisdom, not being greedy, anything.

Now tell the kids to write a fable illustrating that lesson.

Maybe let the kids decide whether these should go home. If they want to send them home, how about having the kids illustrate them, and letting the "package" be a handsome one? What they're trying to communicate will have a readier audience that way.

Tall Tale Contests

Deloris Blount likes to run "tall tale" contests in her classroom, and loves the motivation that the challenge of a contest imparts.

The idea: write a tall tale—that is, something that's simply not true. Can it be about yourself? Yes. Can it be about an invented character? Of course. Can it be (with permission, before the writing and after) about another student in the class, a friend? Why not?

But the tale must be a lie from beginning to end. I think it's a good idea to say something like, "Anyone who says anything true in these stories will be penalized!"

The prize for the biggest liar? Something small.

Did the whole class participate with alacrity? Give them all a prize, and tell them it was just impossible to choose a winner. That gets you off the hook, and creates a "no-loser" situation.

Story Line: You Start It, They Finish It

This one is simple, yet effective for kids who have a tough time starting.

The idea is that you provide the first line to the story. You might provide a single one, or a list from which to choose. You might make up simple sentences of your own, such as:

> The huge tree fell.
> Carlos filled the glass with milk.
> The window shattered so loudly it woke me.

Or, alternately, you might take a line which begins a famous book:

> "Now what I want is Facts." (Dickens)
> "Call me Jonah." (Vonnegut)
> "It was a bright cold day in April, and the clocks were striking thirteen." (Orwell)

The kids take it from there.

Variation: Kids Starting It

In this variation, the kids themselves choose the first lines of the story. They either make them up (teacher at the board, recording) or on a scholarly search find from the library particularly striking first lines from existing novels or short stories. The search in itself can be a book-opening, eye-opening activity!

Double Negative Story

The concept of double negatives needs to be taught or reinforced before you launch into this activity.

After all (or a great majority) of kids understand what makes a double negative, pass out paper, scissors, construction paper, and crayons. Make a stapler available.

Have the kids make mini-notebooks that say "Double Negatives" on the front. Their task will be to circulate in the halls during passing period, in the yard and cafeteria during lunch time, and go wherever they need to go to overhear double negatives. These they write down.

After two days of this, most kids will have a pretty good collection.

Now tell the kids that they are to take their double negative notebooks and write a story in which all of their overheard double negatives are included. Suggest that they use many of them in dialogue—it's easier.

In case there are some kids who claim they didn't overhear nothing, have them make up some double negatives for use in the story.

Double Negative Story Extension

After the story is finished, you may want to have the kids *rewrite* the story, straightening out each double negative. This is a good grammar exercise, and kids attack it with alacrity.

Who, What, Where, and When: Pot Luck

Mary Anne Wold likes to use this one:

The teacher puts the following words on the board: *Who, What, When, Where, Why,* and *How.* He or she talks with the class, discussing why these elements are important in the telling of any story—be that story a newspaper article or a short piece of fiction. Examples may be drawn from a story or articles you've read together lately.

Now, kids take out a piece of paper and fold it into four sections. They tear the paper at the folds. Once piece becomes four pieces.

Each small piece is folded in half now. On the outside of the first is written *Who.* On the second, *What.* On the third, *Where.* On the fourth, *When*

114

Now, one by one, the student opens the papers and writes something appropriate. In the *Who* might be Gilgamesh or Ronald Reagan. In the *What* might be something completely unrelated, such as *falls in love with a beautiful Mexican girl*, or *discovers a way to grow hair wherever you want it.* Under *Where* might be *on the dark side of the moon*, or *the Potomac River. When* could be *1422 B.C., 1991 A.D.,* or perhaps *last Tuesday night.* The kids will have fun choosing these.

Have one kid collect the *Who* papers and mix them up. Do the same for the *What* papers, the *Where*, and the *When.* Mix all in their separate stacks.

Now pass 'em out, each kid receiving one of each category, not receiving any of his or her own creation.

The task: *Write a story using the papers in front of you as central to your plot. What about the **why** and the **how**? That's up to you! Surprise us!*

Caution: no foul language or body function humor.

Cracking the Personal Ad Codes

This activity can be done either with a single personal ad from the newspaper, or from a collection that you glean over the months or years.

In this case we're not talking about those personal ads where someone is looking for a lover. We're talking about those weird, cryptic ones in the Sunday paper—the ones that go something like this:

> Rosie–Mike's O.K. The daffodils bloom. Not all cars were on fire. Want to know if there's anything left in the jar. Answer ASAP. We're running out of breath.

You can guess what this activity involves: creating a story out of these wild, only partially informative ads. Kids are great at leaps of imagination, and detective work appeals greatly.

If you should happen to have a few of these, or, better, enough to supply each kid with one, great. But be sure that kids get a chance to share their sleuth-work (hypotheses) with the class.

Group-work is great here, too, as long as it results in either individual or collective writing.

International Music/International Writing

This activity takes a bit of research on the part of the teacher. Once you have the information, it can be used in future years.

First, get a record of music native to a certain country. Let's use the Soviet Union as an example. Let's say you've purchased a record of Russian ballads. This is a good choice, for it is unlikely that anyone in the class speaks Russian. So the kids won't know what the men and women in the record are singing, right?

O.K. Now the teacher goes to the library and does a bit of research, making a list of names of: Soviet cities and towns; Soviet male first names and female first names; and prominent geographical places such as rivers, lakes, mountains, seas. Those *really* into the research might compile a list of Soviet foods, names of automobiles, and individual, well-explained city landmarks such as Red Square or the Kremlin.

All of the lists fit on a ditto sheet or a sheet to be reproduced in some other way.

On the day of this activity, the teacher gets the dittos ready to pass out, but waits a bit.

Now the teacher plays the Russian music until the first kid begins to show a glimmer (glummer?) of boredom.

At this point, the teacher passes out the information sheet.

The kids are asked to write a story using Russian characters (names chosen from list) in a place (see list) and using any other information from the sheet.

How do the kids get a focus on how to go about beginning?

Focus on a song the class chooses as a favorite, and play it repeatedly. Ask the kids to imagine what the singers are saying, and relate it to the words found on the list you have passed out.

This activity, seemingly complicated, works well. A *mood* emerges from the music, and real stories can spring from *feeling!*

Visualization

Visualization is a method vastly underexplored in our schools.

There are many mutations, but one example might go like this:

The teacher asks the kids to take out a clean piece of paper, then turns out the classroom lights. The teacher asks the kids—yes, all of them—yes, high schoolers, too—to put their heads down and close their eyes. The teacher might have played music as an introduction to this activity, but not necessarily.

Now, the classroom completely silent, the teacher begins a soothing monologue. Something like this:

> *You are walking home from school alone. In the space of one moment, you are suddenly not walking the street anymore—you are in a grassy field. The field is huge, and there is a slight warm breeze. Can you feel that breeze across your face? It's so soothing—it makes you feel as if you're on vacation.*
>
> *You continue to walk across the field. The soil gives in just a little under your feet as you walk. That feels good.*

118

*At the other end of the field there
are some trees. See their green leaves
blowing in the wind? How huge those
trees are! I think they're poplar trees!*

*There seems to be a woman wav-
ing to you from under the largest tree.
You get a good feeling when you look at
her. What is she wearing? I can't see if
she's waving because she's happy or
because she is concerned.*

*Get closer, now, and find out. She
is saying something to you, and you are
answering her. Now you are having a
conversation. Is that laughter I hear, or
crying? It's so hard for me to hear. But
you know. Now you are together, sitting
down in the tall grass and talking. What
are you talking about?*

Of course, you've insisted that the kids not talk: just
listen and imagine.

Now you ask the kids to put their heads up again,
and, you guessed it, write about the situation and
conversation.

Encourage the kids not simply to report the conversation they "heard" but to give very specific details. Who
is this person? Why meet in the field? What was the conversation about? What background led to that conversation? What will the future of the situation be?

These responses, according to either your wishes or those of the kids, can come either in prose or in poetry.

There *will* be some kids who draw a blank. In their case, simply ask them to "make it up—pretend those things happened to you." For the other kids, you'll get the sensation of having really connected.

If possible, keep the mood pensive by not turning on the lights during the first-draft writing of this activity (assuming you have windows!)

Jane Leonard recommends a guided imagery book published by The Learning Works called *Dream Scenes*. A book like this would be great for those days when your own imagination is unable to locate, having taken off a few days ago for Chichen-Itza, Mexico.

Variation: Visualization

Being careful not to choose either a class clown or a jerk, choose a volunteer student to do the visualization narrative.

It is important that the teacher already have run through this at least once prior to a student's guiding the class through the activity.

There must be a million variations of visualization. Kids like it tremendously, not only because it gives them specific pictures and textures, but also because, in this safe and quiet environment, they can relax.

Story Stolen from Titles

The teacher's job: either go to the *Titles* appendix at the end of this book, or get one or two anthologies of stories and poems. If a few current literary magazines are available, these are great, too.

Now, on the board or on a ditto sheet, list at least twenty-five titles, going not only for prosaic ones ("The Confession") but for wilder ones too ("Investigation of a Young Dog").

The kids' challenge: to try to weave as many of these titles as possible into a short story that makes sense.

Offer the prize of a gum drop (or some such token acknowledgment) to the kid who includes the most titles in a story; also be happy with kids who aren't having such an easy time, but are trying nonetheless. This kind of writing is good for certain kinds of thinkers, it seems; others have a tougher time.

Therefore, be generous with examples of your own that draw from the same titles:

"It's been good to know you, said the tall woman as she was *picking cherries, "Hollywood* was fun—better than a *Russian history lesson . . ."* and on.

A second draft of this activity is a good place for kids to peer-edit. What made no sense? What could be changed to fit better? Since many of the words are already someone else's, there's little personal affront taken at suggestions for change on these.

Mystery Woman, Mystery Dog: You Solve It

During the last school year, teachers actually got this note in their mailboxes:

> TO STUDENTS AND FACULTY:
> If you happen to have seen a black and white dalmatian dog on a leash with a blonde lady holding the leash yesterday, March 27, after school by the Chestnut Street fence, please see me as soon as possible. Thank you.
>
> Mr. Sui
> (Dean)

Teachers were asked to read this note to classes. I never did find out what the mystery woman and dog were up to, but what a fun fiction-making exercise!

The task for the teacher: pretend. Use this note, change the name of the writer, and get the kids in your class to write little vignettes explaining the lady, her dog, her suspicious behavior at the "Chestnut Street fence [fill in your street]," and reasons for said behavior.

This activity can be a very simple one—good for basic classes. Even one paragraph can be speculative, and a full-blown story may not be desired here.

Descriptive Writing: Classroom Props

This is easy, and kids like it. Before class, assemble five or ten numbers written on cards. One number to a card. Now look around the classroom to unlikely things, obvious things, common things, strange things which may be described. Tape a number to each of these things.

The kids will come in and notice the numbers. They'll ask you what they're for. Tell them it's a secret; whet the appetite.

At the appropriate time, tell the kids to take out paper. Write "Descriptive Writing" on the board and explain what it means. Point out the numbers, and ask if anyone can guess what they're for. Some kids will get it — they're supposed to describe the objects.

But: the objects must be described without the object's name itself being used. Kids can describe its size (rulers encouraged), shape, function, feel, what other object it might resemble, and so on. Encourage *exhausting* the description before starting to describe another.

With younger kids, this is a great way to either introduce or reinforce *simple sentences*. Help the kids start simple sentences: "Object number two is round. It has numbers on it," etc.

To avoid crowding around objects, have some kids start with #1, some with #5, some with #10, as needed.

123

This activity can take a number of days and, if used appropriately, can teach a lot.

Final hint: use both things easy to describe (the chalkboard) and things tougher to describe (pencil sharpener, Picasso print, etc.)

Variation #1: Descriptive Writing: Classroom Props

Do this activity with things brought from your home. Try still-life sorts of things: painted plates, vases, apples, bananas, roses, anything.

Variation #2: Descriptive Writing: Classroom Props

After you've done this once, wait some time and try it in groups. The "detective" feeling arises here. Encourage absolutely accurate description. Tell the kids you're a Martian who has no idea what these things are, and you need them described perfectly. In groups, it is permissible for all members of the group (four is best) to have the same work on their respective papers.

Variation #3: Descriptive Writing: Classroom Props

Some months later you may want to get the kid-groups themselves to each decide upon one numbered "prop" for the class to write on.

Kids themselves can bring from home things to be described.

Warning: this activity can be run into the ground. Better to do two than three, it seems.

Object Number Three

Object number three is a poster. It has a rectangular shape. It has a smooth, flat, shiny surface. There's a woman holding a fan. The fan has a ruffled surface. The fan is colored yellowish and dark blue. The fan has a word on it. The word is "Carmen." The word is colored ravishing red. She has long, black hair. A purple flower is on top of her head. She has a black dress on. She has a nice tan on her skin.

In the background, there's a bridge. The bridge is colored beige. The bridge looks like it has a rough surface. The bridge has two lamp poles on each side of it. The poles are colored black. The poles have four-sided glasses on them. In the glass there is a lamp or bulb. The bulb is sitting on an arch. The arch is colored light brown. Between the sides of the bridge there are small columns. There are about 24 to 44 columns. The bridge looks old and needs to be re-painted. The paint should be colored red.

Going back to the woman, she has a Flamenco veil. The Flamenco veil is colored black. On the upper half of the veil is a yellowish color. She is wearing red lipstick. She has a little bit of facial make-up. The facial make-up is colored light peach. She has sexy brown eyes.

Beyond the bridge there are trees. The trees' leaves are colored a gorgeous green. The leaves have a smooth, silky texture.

—Greg Cabig

Title Tyrannies: Prose

Since prose allows for less "field" work and is therefore less "open" than poetry, please take caution not to be in the least prosaic in the selection of titles you choose for prose creative writing activities.

There is a clear difference between this activity and the construction of an *essay* as it is interpreted by American public schools. An essay found in a typical minimum-standards test is almost by definition unimaginative, dry, and predictable, leaving little room for creative "flight."

This activity, however, needs to be crazy in order to have life.

It goes like this. The teacher creates some titles and has the kids write on those titles. The titles can be "How-To," such as: "How to Build a Three-Story House for a Potato Bug." "How without Moving to Stop a Swing from Swinging in the Wind," "How to Make the Rain Stop" (Don't accept "Wait."). "How to Get from San Francisco to the Virgin Islands without a Map," and many more.

This will, of course, yield a certain kind of prose, that in instructional form.

Another kind of prose assignment is to select an essay topic from one of the many books filled with topics for essays. But change them! Know that if the topic doesn't interest you it won't interest the kids, and the papers will sit on your desk uncorrected until the millennium.

127

Take one of those typical titles, twist it, and change it. "Good Nutrition" might be altered to "Good Nutrition for Banana Slugs."

Make it fresh! Interesting to kids!

Describe Yourself: Three Ways

This activity is good for putting kids in someone else's shoes, for giving them a wider perspective on themselves, and for giving them new physical perspectives from which to ponder things.

The task: describe yourself from the perspectives of at least three different people. A single paragraph from each "voice" might be sufficient.

Sample "voices" might be: a parent, a little or big brother or sister, a friend, an enemy, a teacher, a stranger on the street, or the storekeeper.

One student did a wonderful perspective, describing himself from the point of view of his dog.

Encourage that the students write not just about personality perceptions here, but also *spatial* perspectives. (The dog example would be good in illustrating this.) Also, don't forget *humor*! How dry this activity would be without a light touch!

Family Photographs

There's an immediate advantage to activities using family photographs, and an immediate problem.

The advantage is that using family photos is a very high-interest vehicle for getting kids to write.

The problem is that not all kids *have* family photos, or, if they exist at home, not all kids have parents who will take the time to fish out appropriate snapshots.

So that means that family snapshot activities are best done on a 100 percent class basis, or at home, or as an independent in-class project.

An alternative is for the *teacher* to provide a few "family" photos—groups of people in a situation—for kids who come with no pictures.

Activities can vary. Choose one person from a family photograph and write from her perspective. Speak to us in *her* voice. Tell us what's on her mind. Tell us why she's wearing the red flowered dress. Why does she (Why do *you*) love that dress? What important things in your life have happened in that dress? What is the future for you? And so forth.

Or: simply *describe* the photo in as much detail as possible. "*Three people are standing in front of a fire hydrant: a tall man, a boy of about thirteen, and a short dark-haired woman who appears to be the boy's mother. The man is wearing a gray hat. He has a cigarette in his mouth, and his upper lip is stained with nicotine. They are looking at something that is not the camera. It seems to be in the distance."* You get the picture.

Or: Write about *yourself* in a family photograph. When is this? What are you doing? Why are you there? How are you feeling? Is something about to happen? What do you remember?

Or: Write a complete lie about the photo, who's in it, and what's going on.

Or: Exchange photographs, and write either a complete lie about what's going on—and who the people are— or make an educated guess as to those and other things.

Or: change ages. Make the kid the parent to the adults. Give him language—a dialogue ensues between them. What are the sources of their worries and anger?

Or: See? So many possibilities.

And in what form? Poetry? Prose?

Photos lend themselves to poems very easily. Try that, perhaps.

For more descriptive work, maybe prose, maybe poetry, or maybe experiment with prose-poems. (See the Césaire prose-poem in the appendix.)

Finally, this is a good springboard to get the kids to invent imaginary dialogues. A single photo can be the start of a fantastic dialogue—or even a short play.

What rich artifacts photographs are!

Snowball Sentences (Rhopalisms)

This activity is best done with a dictionary on the desk, though some particularly erudite students have the ability to do it without the dictionary.

A snowball sentence is a sentence that starts with a one-letter word and adds a letter to each successive word.

Here's one:

> *I do not ever drive slowly, because maniacal velocities corroborate contemporary civilization's understandable annihilationism.*

and another:

> *O he sat long, sadly, hardly talking, spitting, pensively ruminating theoretical speculations, demonstrating specifically disassimilating postintoxicative antisociabilities.*

Perhaps shorter sentences are in order for kids! There are a few challenges here: to create sentences which, while a little wild, are nonetheless grammatical; to put a number of them together into a paragraph that makes sense; and, for really committed kids, to string as many as possible together and form a basic, if crazy, story.

Warning: not for easily frustrated groups—you'll have a revolution on your hands.

Excerpts from the Preposterous Dictionary

If you're having a difficult time getting kids to know what a dictionary entry looks like, how a pronunciation key is used, or how dictionaries contain parts of speech, try this activity.

Each student gets or shares a dictionary and opens it to a place of her or his choice. The student will notice that words are broken into syllables, are written in a pronunciation key, are assigned a part of speech, and are defined.

The kid's job is to make entries from her own Preposterous Dictionary. The task: to make up words—double-checking that these words do not exist—then syllabicate them, helping the reader by using the standard pronunciation key, assigning them a part of speech, then defining the words in descending order of frequency of usage.

This, for some kids, could evolve into quite a project, culminating perhaps in the publication of a "book."

A more moderate approach is to get kids to do a dozen or so each, then to choose a few students to alphabetize them, then, if the energy still remains, to run off a classwide Preposterous Dictionary.

Fun.

Excerpts from the
Preposterous Dictionary

Chuk \ chuk \ v.t.
1. To punch someone continuously. *The boy chuked me cruelly.*
2. To punch an armadillo at midnight. *We chuked the animal just as he was about to attack us.*

—**Selwyn Au**

Show—Don't Tell: Description

We often exhort our kids in writing to show—not tell. Larry Prager likes to force the kids' hands on this, by giving them an opening sentence, such as *The sun was hot.*

The kids must take off from there, turning that statement into a *showing* paragraph. How did it feel? Who was there, and what was going on in reaction to the sun's heat?

Requirement: the word *hot* must not be used again at any time within the paragraph.

Variation: Show—Don't Tell

Certainly the subject doesn't have to be the sun and its heat, but extremes do seem to work best in this activity. Cold, high, low, boring, angry, stupid, joyous, bright, hungry, strong, weak, and other extremes work well.

Do try to avoid bland introductory descriptors such as pretty, beautiful, nice, kind, and so on; these tend to offer little the kids can grab hold of, and flaccid writing will result.

Newspaper Article: The Big Lie

If you have access to newspapers at your school, good. If not, this activity can still be done well.

Pass out a stack of newspapers. Ask the kids to read through them, picking out specific articles that interest them. After they settle on one, tell the kids to read the article carefully.

Collect the newspapers.

The kids are now asked to write an article themselves, *but* there can be no truth to it. The article must contain only lies and ridiculously inflated exaggerations.

Remember to remind the kids that the *who, what, where, why* and *how* are important to good journalism.

Humor is to be encouraged!

Variation: Newspaper Article

No newspapers? It's O.K. Either read the kids an article that might get their attention, or simply talk about what's important in a typical newspaper article (see above). Then let the kids go to it with some big lies.

Extension: Newspaper Article

After the class has completed the project of writing preposterous articles, either you yourself or the kids should assemble the writing into a class "newspaper." If the works have not yet been read aloud, great surprises will be in store.

To facilitate this assembling, you might think about having kids do their final draft on ditto paper (maybe two to a ditto where possible) and running them off.

Some fine writing will come of this, and, if you're like me, newspaper articles forevermore will take on an aura of unreality.

Phony Genealogies

This activity is similar to the fake biographical report.

Kids are asked to make genealogies of their own family.

Not a word of truth is allowed, but a complete description—physical, psychological, etc.—is encouraged.

This project can last a long time, can be extended into the distant past, and is great on the interest scale.

By all means, at the end, have the kids draw a family tree!

Family Tree

My family tree isn't really interesting. First of all, my great-great-great-great-great grandpa was a raw sewage dealer. He dealt with the Japanese, the Russians, the Germans, and many other countries. His wife worked in the coal mines and every day she would come out of the mines with twenty pounds of dirt all over her.

136

My great-great-great-great grandpa married an Italian. They opened a shop called "Patel's Pizzeria." No wonder they got sick of mushrooms!

My great-great-great grandpa lived in the forest. Since they had no TV, they spent their time talking to nature. They played games with the animals. The bear would always win at checkers.

My great-great grandparents lived in Canada. My great-great grandpa used to make wine for horses, and his wife would sit around and drink it.

My great grandpa won the smallest Nobel Prize in chemistry. He made a liquid solution that shrinks your appetite—and you. Before he knew that, he tested it on himself. That's why he got the smallest Nobel Prize.

My grandfather worked on a farm in Belgium. He had a pig that could win races, a rooster that cocked loud, and a horse that climbed up trees.

My father is a foot doctor. He takes X-rays, checks toes and heels, and massages feet. Me, I'm really a superhero. My name is Batgame! I fight for all rights for Nintendo. I've won a lot of games, so don't mess around with me!

And that is my (phony) family tree.

—**Nimish Patel**

The Phony Research Report: Model-Based

I suppose we all give kids "report" assignments. You know, the usual school report about a person or place. Typical.

Have the kids do one of these early in the year, and, once you correct it, make sure they (or you) keep it.

Soon after the real report is done, and using the "true" report as a model, have the kids write an equally complicated phony report, based on their conception of a person or place that never existed. This can really be fun. When was this person born? Where? (Why?) What were the conditions of this person's childhood? Where did she/he live? What was her/his life like? How did this person distinguish herself/himself? When did death occur? Where? How?

A similar pattern of questions can be used for the *place* report.

If the character is based on a literary model, why not have the student write some poems written by their fictional character? Or a short story, a play, or any excerpts from such?

Remember, *humor* is the greatly desired by-product here. An activity like this without humor would be dry indeed.

Many kids get into illustrating their usual, traditional reports. Why not illustrate this one?

Archaeology:
Relics and Artifacts

George Patterson likes to do this activity in Social Studies, but it would be equally exciting in English.

The class is introduced to the concept of *artifacts*. Artifacts made thousands of years ago are discovered by modern archaeologists. Those archaeologists theorize as to their use and meaning to the people who made them. Some of these *theories* may be true, and some may be pure baloney. "When researchers are in doubt," George says, "the artifact becomes a 'religious' object." (I love that comment.)

Here's what the teacher says to the kids:

You are an archaeologist in the year 6892. You have encountered some objects from your (real, present) home or school environment. Describe the object without naming it. Describe what the object was used for in the year it was used. Be very specific—like a scientist!—in your description. And, of course, be wrong!

Kids like this. Help them out, maybe, with "pre-civilization" examples: telephones, Barbie dolls, trash cans, pens, telephone poles, bifocal eyeglasses, on and on.

They'll enjoy sharing their discoveries with the class.

September 9, 6892

I have returned from the excavation site in San Francisco and have found many interesting ancient artifacts which have been dated around the late twentieth century. My findings may help recreate the life and culture of San Francisco before Iraq mercilessly bombed the city after falsely declaring peace, starting World War III.

We have carefully uncovered a skeleton of a toddler. Its skull is wrapped in plastic and it is clear that plastic headwear was highly fashionable in those primitive times. The child was trying to remove the plastic from its head during its death.

We have also found a metal object. It is 1 centimeter wide, 13 cm long, and egg-shaped on one end. This egg shape is about 4 cm wide. It is my opinion and my fellow archaeologists' alike that this was used to cover a precious toenail, thereby protecting the nail from dirt and injury. It is now being manufactured and will be marketed worldwide.

There is one object we are not very sure of. It is U-shaped and is about the size of an adult rear-end. My fellow archaeologists think it was used as protective headgear, but personally, I think it was a form of currency.

—**Ronald Cruz**

Tongue Twisters

Who doesn't like to play around with words that glue themselves to the tongue? How often do we actually *think* of our tongues doing their contortions?

Kids love to write tongue twisters, and it can be the best and easiest way to teach *alliteration* and *assonance*.

I usually start the class out by going into my own memory of tongue twisters; write them on the board and get the class to try saying them. Then, in asking the class if anyone knows any tongue twisters, I'm usually surprised at the new ones that come forth.

The teaching has begun: repeating consonants and vowels, mostly, though *toy boat* defies logic.

Write just one tongue twister? Naw—the kids will want to do many more, and will just be getting warmed up when the good ones start being invented.

At the end, how about not only a performance of tongue twisters, but, for tomorrow, the teacher having ready for the kids a dittoed "anthology" of the class's best twisters? And now, a contest to see who can stand before the class and get 'em all?

I Am the Camera

This is another *focus* activity—this time with a simple mechanical device. But not *too* mechanical.

The kids cut a standard, blank, white piece of paper in half or quarters. In the middle of their individual piece of paper, each student cuts or punches a *small* (quarter-inch maximum) square or circle.

This is his "aperture."

Now, the task is to choose one thing to focus on and describe. But not just describe. *Describe.*

Since the chosen object will be smaller than small and the distraction of the larger "field" diminished, urge the kids to hold their papers steady, fix on one object, commit themselves to it, and describe it in the most minute detail.

Perhaps one student is focusing on another student's eye. Saying "I see a light-brown eye" is nowhere near enough. Have you ever really *looked* at an eye? There are many different shapes—ovals and circles—and an overwhelming swirl of colors outside what might be a jet black pitlike circle. An eye has *texture, shape, color,* and *motion.* So much can be described!

There are many possible objects on which to focus. But to up the interest ante, you might bring in a few small objects from home. A screw, a moldy piece of cheese, lint from the dryer, a charcoaled ember from the fire, a dead insect, a fragment of a photograph, or so forth.

This activity can be done singly or in two's or three's: one focuser/describer and one writer/recorder (then switch). Or, in doing detailed observations of, say, aspects of a face, a threesome including the observer, the observed, and the recorder of the observer's spoken words. Then the kids rotate roles.

A Panoply of Diaries

A fictional diary can be a wonderful way of engaging the imagination of your students. Fictional diaries can be written from so many points of view! The characters can be historical, necessitating a certain amount of research; current events–based, also necessitating research of a different kind; or, finally, strictly fantastic creations.

If you ask your kids to write fictional diaries, be certain to give them a few keys: ask them to describe using the five senses, to tell *stories* of what is happening in their lives, to give the reader a good sense of *place*, and to allow the reader a glimpse into the innermost *feelings* of the diarist.

Here are some sample diary subjects. You'll do fine inventing your own as well.

- Diary of a Madman or Madwoman
- Diary of a Soldier
- Diary of a Pilgrim
- Diary of a Terrorist
- Diary of a Healer
- Diary of a President
- Diary of a Pioneer

- Diary of a Rich Person
- Diary of a particular historical character

Variation: Diary

What about diary of an animal? A rock? A blade of grass? The left front tire of an automobile? A *Playboy* magazine on a drugstore rack? A quart of milk?

All these, and many more diaries of everyday objects, will engage kids.

Diary of a Pilgrim

November 16, 1642

It was dawn when I woke up at 4:00 A.M. in my cabin. Today was the beginning of a whole different life. I am going to sail to the New World. My family and three other families will be sailing on a small wooden ship with us. By 5:30 A.M. everyone was aboard and we set sail. The air was cool and once in a while a breeze blew by me. I played ball with the rest of the children while the women were in the kitchen cooking or knitting. All the men were too busy paddling the oars. The whole day was sunny and breezy. Everybody couldn't have a big meal because we must conserve our food for the long journey. Once a day we must only have two very small meals. By night everybody had a peaceful sleep while four men were on guard.

—Loretta Basco

Recipe for an Enemy

Most kids are familiar with recipes. If you doubt this, bring in some real recipes yourself and read them as an introduction to the activity.

Now give the kids time to concentrate singly and write a recipe for an enemy. Ask them to think of the most disgusting/poisonous/vile/revolting ingredients and processes.

Make sure the kids write not only the recipe's ingredients, but also method of preparation and manner of proper serving.

Peer proofread (be ready for guffaws and theatrical retching), do a second draft, collect the work. Read these on an empty stomach: Roach Eye Stew Served over Steaming Maggots can quease the best of us on a bad day.

Wimpy Variation: Recipe

Same thing in reverse. This is a recipe for someone dearly loved; however, no real food can be called for. Get the kids to think of the things they themselves most treasure. Encourage them to put these together in a credible, recipe-like format to serve to their loved one—mother, brother, lover.

Younger kids generally keep these directed toward a family member or best friend. Older kids sometimes get a little racy on this one, so be aware of this before you assign it.

Roach Eye Stew

To my worst enemy. I made this
recipe just for you.

5   cups of sewer water
½   cup of smashed roach eyes
1   lb. of dandruff
6   turtle eggs
1¼ minced frog tongues
40 spiders (with legs)
1   pot of steamed maggots

First you let the sewer water come to
a boil, then add the dandruff. Mix the
turtle eggs with the shells, add frog
tongues and spiders and roach eyes. Let
it simmer for 20 minutes then serve over
steamed maggots.

—**Marcus Davis**

Automatic Writing

I've heard many different definitions of *automatic writing*. This is what in my classroom I call "automatic writing."

Have the kids clear their desks of all books and notebooks; they should have either a single blank sheet of paper or their writing folder, ready to go. In their hand should be a pen or pencil. My instructions:

> We're going to do something called "automatic writing." It's a lot of fun — don't be worried. Here are the rules. I'm going to put a word up on the board. Then I'm going to set my timer for three minutes, and say "Go!" In that three minutes, I want you to write as much as you can about that word. Don't worry about complete sentences or spelling or grammar or seriousness — just write whatever comes into your mind. Easy? There's a catch! I forgot to tell you the most important rule! It's this: during the entire three minutes, you can't lift your pen or pencil off the page except to go to the next line! Does that mean your words will run together? Yes! Does that mean that your paper will be pretty sloppy? Yes! Just remember: the pen stays on the paper no matter what — it can only come off to skip lines! If you get stuck for a minute, and you can't think of anything on the subject, then write the same word

over and over until you're unstuck!
Ready? On your marks, get set . .

Oops! I forgot to write the word
on the board! O.K. — here it is! (I write
sweet, *or something similarly simple.)*
On your marks, get set, go!

It's great fun, different, and sometimes yields some very interesting writing. Kids like very much to read aloud what they've written in this crazy, stream-of-consciousness period. Sometimes automatic writing yields "keepers": snatches of writing that can be used elsewhere, later.

Automatic writing is something I repeat a few times a year — not simply because kids like it. My own primary reason for using it is that it serves to lubricate the kids toward other writing that same day. It's short — just a few minutes — and it's a great loosener. If automatic writing takes, say, five minutes, there's still the better part of an hour for other creative writing you might be working on.

CHAPTER FOUR

Poetry or Prose: You Choose

It's often difficult to break down activities into clear genres. Often the predisposition of the student will determine what form — poetry or prose — the work will take. Length may have something to do with it, and width too!

Many of the activities listed on the following pages can be channelled by the *teacher* or the *writer* in the direction of either poetry or prose.

Finally, many activities have ready variations in the other form. The sound effects set, for example, is very different in prose form and poetry form, as are the "found story" and "found poem" activities.

Poetry or prose? the decision is yours, or it may be the kids' as a group, or it may be left up to individuals. Or yet another variation may be suggested by kids, and that variation may far surpass anything in this book. Let's keep our ears open!

Myth-Making: Poetry or Prose

This activity can be done by students either in prose form or in poetry.

It seems O.K. to let the student herself choose the form.

Ideally, the teacher will have introduced the activity over a period of days or weeks by having had the kids study actual myths. Edith Hamilton is great, as is d'Aulaire. African folktales also are spectacularly good for this writing activity.

The concept is simple. The student herself gets an idea to explain a particular natural phenomenon or human behavior, such as "Why the Sun Rises in the East," or "Why Rivers are Crooked," or "Why Raccoons Have Claws," or "Why Humans Don't Eat Lying Down," or "How Diseases Came to Earth," or a thousand other possibilities, best if conceived by the student.

The writer invents a story to fit. In *myths*, it might involve a god or gods. The *folktale* might not involve a god. The teacher might make a stipulation of choice here, or just leave the kids alone.

Do remember that such stories often describe be-havior, and they don't go too far afield. I would discourage a student from simply saying, "Rivers once ran straight, then an alien from space came and made them crooked." That's lazy work.

Preferable, and worth emphasizing, is that in a myth of this sort, the river—and important actors near the river,

POETRY OR PROSE: YOU CHOOSE

possibly human, possibly animal—are given a special *life*, and their *behavior*, either benign or malevolent, is what has caused some higher power to alter those rivers.

You'll have good success with this one, and your reading of the papers will be of high interest for you!

Why the Sun Is the Greatest Star

Many billions of years ago, while God was making our universe, all the created planets in our solar system always liked to make fun of the sun, which was the smallest and dimmest star.

The sun hated all the insults but couldn't get away from them, because he was stuck in the middle of all the other planets.

He asked to see the creator, God, to ask if He could do anything about his smallness and dimness. God agreed to make him the greatest star. He would warm the other planets with his brilliant light.

The sun didn't know what to do. He didn't want to help his enemies. He agreed even though he was not happy about it.

God made him the greatest star as promised, and the planets were too afraid to make fun of the sun anymore.

—Wendel Tse

Wanted: In Poetry or Prose

We've all seen those personal ads in the paper. A man advertises for a woman (certain requirements) or a woman advertises for a man. Or a man advertises for a man and a woman advertises for a woman. Or a man advertises for a man and a woman and a woman advertises . . . you get it.

If we shift gears a bit, tone things down some, kids can write such ads too.

This activity is one, really, that tries to get kids to give words to their emotions.

The teacher advertises the activity like this:

> *If you could put a "Wanted" ad in the paper for a certain kind of person to love or to love you, how would you word it? The person certainly does not have to be someone your own age. It could be an adult who might give you some kind of love you feel you're not getting right now. Or, it might not necessarily be love you need—it might just be understanding, or something else.*
>
> *Write an ad in which you try to reach out to someone who might be able to supply what you want. Remember—describe what you want in detail—give situations you might like—be descriptive!*

This activity is safest done anonymously—no names on paper, and/or papers handed in only at the desire of students.

Caution against obscenity; advocate sincerity. The writing that ensues might be indeed wonderful for the kids.

Want Ad Variation: Poetry

In this want ad, get the kids to warm up by using *real* personal ads as a way to create "found" poetry. Get an alternative newspaper or two, cut out as many ads as you have students, and distribute them randomly.

Now, get the kids to break the phrases found in the ads into lines of poetry, the art here being their choice of exactly where to break the lines:

SWM, 36, hungry
for companionship,
hopes you read
this ad & weep
with recognition
of our most incredible
connection
since you like TV
walks on sunny beaches
in the snow throwing snow-
balls & I like
stuff
like
that too so
(blah blah blah . .)

Then, after the kids have had a chance to do this and share their "line" discoveries, have them write a *fictional* personal ad, integrating parts of the "model" while making up ideas of their own and breaking down the lines into poetry.

That's a mouthful, but you get it.

Teenage Date

S.B.C.C. (small, but cute chic), looking for a gorgeous, rich, dude who lives in a beach house in Florida. Searches for someone that wants to have fun and likes playing around. Also someone that can surf and dress well. Someone who is daring, goes to movies, and has a good sense of humor. He must be cool, trendy, and jammin. Besides being fun to be with, he must be understanding, smart, responsible, sensible, serious and demanding at times. Someone that has good taste and likes going to the beach, mall, and movies.

I am a small, but cute chic who just wants to have fun. I have long brown hair with a body wave. I have chestnut-brown eyes and I have a pretty cute smile. I love hanging around malls, beaches, movies, and everywhere else. My favorite sports and hobbies are swim ming, shopping, talking on the phone,

and having fun. I may be gullible at
times, but I'm also trendy, cute, understanding, weird, and loving. I talk with a
Canadian valley accent and mostly eat at
Mickey D's. I have a sort of changing
attitude; but I'm mostly happy. I also enjoy dancing, going to school, cruisin
around with friends and more. I love
using credit cards, especially if they are
not mine! (TRIX) Even though I'm an
ordinary valley-girl, I would love to try
something new. But mostly I'm just a
regular gal that loves to party and live
life the way it was made to be.

—**Mellissa Tolentino**

My Life: Prose

This writing activity has nothing to do with your students' lives.

It asks the students to pick an inanimate object (a rock, a door, a beam in a building, a garbage can, etc.) and describe the life of that object. What is in a day for that thing? How does it feel? A tremendous pull of gravity, in the case of the rock? Does time pass the same for the garbage can as it does for us? Are there relationships with other objects?

Encourage the kids to use first person on this one — they'll get "into" their chosen object more completely.

My Life: Poetry

Let the poetry in this activity be spare, sparse, for the speaking by an object is a rare thing, and one would guess that words don't come easy to a stone.

This activity is the same as above; yet, if you choose to have the kids write poems, the tone of the room will be more meditative and specific. That's O.K.!

Let the poem be written in whatever voice the writer wants. No length limit or minimum, but do encourage the kids to become the object itself.

Dream: Poetry or Prose

Ah, dreams. The deep mine, the rich ore.

Kids *love* to write about their dreams, and seldom have a chance to do it. We're so rational, so *conscious* in our classrooms that the rich stuff usually goes ignored, pushed aside.

What to write?

It can start simply. What was your scariest nightmare? What was your happiest dream? It can get more complicated: pick a dream you've had and you'd like to *change*. How would you change it?

How about dream journals? They're rich sources of writing. (Caution here, though. If you try something like this, (1) make *certain* that the student's journal is *absolutely* safe and private, and (2) don't try to analyze a student's dreams. We're not trained for that, and shouldn't pretend we are, no matter how much Jung we've read. This writing is good personally for the kids, but no psychoanalysis here, please!)

What about a poem of dreams? Fine. Lots of possibilities exist, from the creation of dialogues to a multilingual Babel of conversations to single-word descriptions of places, people, and situations.

I like to see the light in kids' eyes when we first introduce writing about dreams. That light seems to say, "My god—I'm going to be able to write about *that dream!* This teacher realizes I have *dreams!*"

Dream Variation: Daydreams

Why not have kids write about their daydreams? Lord knows they have enough of them in school. (Didn't you? Maybe still do now! After buying lottery tickets? How brotherly and sisterly we all are!)

How about having kids write their favorite daydreams? Maybe some will be sexy—and kids won't necessarily want to share those. But there certainly are others that are "lighter" if you don't want to deal with material you feel you might not be able to handle in a class context. I would guess that the younger the student, the lighter the daydreams—but what a false assumption that may be!

Dream: Elephant Woman

I had a weird dream. It started like this:

One day me and my Grandma were strolling down the block, when we came to a red light. I told my Grandma not to go in the street, but she didn't listen. As she was walking across the street, a huge truck came and hit her. She then flew to the sidewalk's curb.

As she was lying helplessly on the curb, another car came and hit her on purpose. He then rammed her again to the curb, and again a third time. I then called the ambulance, and they were on

their way Blood was splattered all over
the place, when to my surprise, my
Grandma got up and looked at me in an
evil way.

I said to my Grandma, "Are you all
right?" And she replied, "Why didn't you
help me?" And as I looked down to get
her purse, she bit me on the arm. I
turned around in fright and started to
run.

As I was running, I ran into a plant
box and fell unconscious. When I looked
up she was right there grinning. I slid
under her legs and ran into a motel. I
didn't notice, but she was right behind. I
then turned around and her head looked
just like the Elephant Man's. I ran into
the bathroom and locked myself in. She
pried the door open with a butter knife
and tried to hit me with it when she got
in.

I started to get tired but I still had
enough energy to put her head in the
toilet. After that I ran into this room and
hid under the covers. I pulled the covers
from over my head and a whole lot of
creatures were on top of me. I screamed,
and I woke up.

—**Alphonso Bryant**

Writing While Being Read To

Perhaps working best in honors classes, this activity requires that students be able to concentrate in a noisy environment.

Students get a partner. One of the partnership gets a book she decides she'd like to read aloud to the other. She begins. The other member is the writer, and as the reader goes on, the writer writes, her *thoughts inspired by what's she's hearing.*

What she writes might be random fragments of thought, complete sentences, or a mix. They might be questions or imperatives. They might be declarations.

This activity can go on for fifteen minutes or so — ten at least — and then the players reverse roles.

You'll be interested in what the kids write in this one — some very focused writing can come of it.

Caution: kids who don't catch on to the exact assignment might believe that this is an assignment in taking notes — it's not, and might more appropriately be titled, "A Penny for Your Thoughts."

Be Someone Else!

Have the kids write a poem from the perspective of another person, or from the perspective of a thing.

"Be Joan of Arc! Or be the president! Or be your mother! Or be a telephone pole! Or a blade of grass! Or a racing motorcycle! Or the moon! Or a broken-down satellite orbiting the earth!"

After you give them a few examples, such as the above, urge kids *not* to use your examples, but to try to come up with their own.

Then, in poetry—or prose, if they're still worried about formal expectations in poetry—have them write it!

Mosquito

Boy am I hungry. I think I'll bite that nice young teenager down there. She looks like the type who might not want me (or any other insect, for that matter) to come near her, so I had better be careful not to let her see me. Okay, I am landed on her arm now. Her blood tastes good. I'm lucky I found such a delicious meal today. There are big holes all around me that humans call *pores*. There are hairs surrounding me that may seem tiny to my victim, but to me they are very tall. What's this? a shadow has just been cast over me. Oh no! There is a hand moving down toward me rapidly! *SLAP!!!*

—**Erika Christie**

Fairytale Rewrites

As its title suggests, this activity simply asks kids to take a fairytale and *change it*.

How? Any way they want. The action of the characters, perhaps. The setting. The conflict. The outcome.

Or the names of the characters. Their age, their motivations. The time they lived in. Some of these, or all, or all of these and more.

Humor and silliness are encouraged!

> *Once there were three-and-a-half big pigs who lived in a high-rise apartment downtown . . .*

Variation: Fairytale Work

Have the kids write a poem using the voice of a particular fairytale figure. What would Rumpelstiltskin want to say if he had a voice, if he could call across the centuries to students in your room? If he could explain *his* side of the story?

The strength of this "your choice" activity is that most kids are familiar with *many* fairytales. Those who aren't can be prodded along with a little extemporaneous storytelling not only on your part, but also on the part of the many volunteer student fairytale tellers!

Effective Sounds

Sound effect records or tapes are great stimulators of writing.

I'm partial to prose work in using sound effect records, but poetry can be exciting here, too.

The idea: the teacher listens to the record ahead of time and becomes familiar with the sounds. (When colleagues walk into your classroom early in the morning and observe you listening to choo-choo trains and race-car engines, tell them you're leaving the profession and are getting reoriented to the sounds of the real world.)

When the kids arrive, the teacher has them clear their desks except for paper and pencils. The teacher might turn out the lights, if the group can handle it. Now, instructions are given: *"I'm going to play some recordings of sounds for you. What I'd like you to do is to listen very carefully to these sounds, and write down what you think they are. Please—no talking—let each student make up his or her own mind as to what sound is being heard. Are you ready? Here we go."*

Now, the teacher plays a single sound, then pauses to allow kids to record their perceptions of what the sound is. (Clearly, a mix between familiar sounds and strange ones is indicated here—more diversity of response results.)

Next? A second sound. Pause for writing. A third. Pause. A fourth, fifth, and maybe sixth.

After six or so sounds have been played, the teacher says, "O.K.: *now you've heard all six sounds. Can anyone*

167

guess what I'm going to be asking you to do? [Guesses are entertained and commended.] Here's your assignment: take these six sounds and weave them into a story.

"Did you hear the sound of a train coming down the tracks? Make that part of your story. Was there a child crying? Make that part of your story. Take your time, let your mind wander, and try your best to get all of these sounds in."

You get it. A couple of comments on this:

Do the kids ask you to play a certain sound again? That's the mark of success—their interest is revving like that race-car engine.

Do you yourself identify most of the sounds to "help" the less auditory kids? That's a disservice to the rest—it creates an orthodoxy for their imaginations.

Ah, the stories you get from this . . . great when read to the class!

Sound Effects Variation: Poetry

This is a little less complicated, and can yield some great poems-from-the-heart.

Same introduction, except you instruct the students to record on their papers what the sound effect makes them feel, see, smell, or taste. Example·

> The train comes down the track.
> Smoke chokes me. The wind of its
> passing almost blows me over.

The next sound now is played, and the same is done.

What is there in the end? Two possible things: either a long poem whose images are dreamlike, or many short poems whose images are evocative by themselves.

Writing to Specific Instrumental Music

Some of the most edifying experiences I've had with kids have been with these activities.

The title of this activity is rather totalitarian—I know. But the concept of "writing to music" has been greatly abused, I think, and I've come to have totalitarian views on this subject. Word has come of teachers putting on Mantovani or Percy Faith or similar elevator music recordings, and saying to kids, "Write whatever you think of." Or of teachers keeping "background music" of similar pasteurized sort droning in the classroom during all "free-writing" periods.

Music is wonderful in the classroom. It helps create a homelike atmosphere, it introduces kids to sounds they may not have heard before, and it definitely can set or maintain a mood. Lovers know that; teachers do, too.

And now the biases in writing with music: no lyrics, and no bad music.

Regarding music with lyrics: have you ever tried to remember how a song goes as another song is playing? It's difficult. So, too, is trying to write *your own* words as other words are being heard or sung. Tough to do.

Regarding music quality, I know this is very subjective. But I think it's safest to stay with music that is exciting or moving: either particular short classical pieces, "world music" instrumentals, or more modern music that is "on the edge" such as Phillip Glass or even John Cage. Here's how I do it:

The Activity

Have the kids clear their desks—except for paper and pencil, then do about five minutes of automatic writing with them. (Please see the description of automatic writing in Chapter Three.)

After that is finished, do not discuss what they've written, but put them off, promising to discuss the automatic writing work later. Now, tell the kids you're going to play a piece of music for them. (Don't tell them that you'll really be playing three or four before the period ends.)

Say something like this:

> *This music probably will be music you've not heard before. As you listen, I bet pictures will come into your mind.*

170

The music will bring images up in your imagination. The music might put you in a different place, and you might imagine having new or strange experiences. Who knows? It might not even be you you imagine—you might see someone else, or experience something no one else in the room can "see." This is you, and we're all different.

As the music plays, write about whatever comes into your mind. Again, don't worry about grammar or spelling—just get it down—we can worry about that other stuff later. I'll only be playing the music one time, so it's important that you write as quickly as possible. If you're stuck, don't worry—something will come, even if it's a "small picture." Here goes.

And the music begins—played on a tape deck or record player as high in fidelity as possible. Play one selection only. Most kids will be writing excitedly. A few might be "frozen." It helps, I think, to walk to those kids individually and ask them if they're stuck. Some will wave you off—they're on their own idea-track. Others will be stuck. With these kids, I make a suggestion: "Maybe for this one start with 'I am . . .'" This usually gets them going.

In about the middle of the music piece, casually walk to the board and write the title and composer. They'll use this to identify their work later.

The writing continues, the music stops. Would they like to hear it again? Most will, and it's reasonable to play

171

the selection once again—kids want to fill out their writing, to keep the images coming. (Yes, in the beginning, I claim the music won't be repeated. This gives them an incentive to "dive in" and get swimming . . .)

Did this first selection seem to be successful? Try another. If the first piece was raucous, tell the kids you're "shifting gears on this next one," and go for something meditative. Same process: the music played twice, but no more.

Three selections usually seems a good limit, though some classes I've worked with have clamored for a fourth.

After the music has ended, kids have the raw material they'll be working from. I ask them immediately—for homework, usually—to begin the second draft/cleanup/ revision process. They arrive in class the next day excited, and ready to read their work publicly.

I love this activity, and find that it combines all the best elements of an ideal teaching and learning situation. You'll be moved by what you witness.

Finally, a mention of music I've found to be quite successful in this work:

- "In the Hall of the Mountain King" by Edvard Grieg
- "Perpetual Motion" by Niccolo Pagannini
- "Gymnopedies #1" by Erik Satie
- "Gnossiennes #4" by Erik Satie
- "Hoedown" from *Rodeo* by Aaron Copland

- "Oxygene, Part 2" by Jean-Michel Jarre
- "The Flight of the Bumblebee" by Nikolai Rimsky-Korsakov
- "The Glass Hall" by Andreas Vollen-weider
- "Meditation" from *Thais* by Jules Massenet
- Other "world music," including South American/Andean instrumental music

Or, if you have one of those twice-in-a-lifetime *wunderkind* classes, try Scene 2 from "Tolstoy" in Philip Glass's *Satyagraha*. It is exquisite. It runs for eleven minutes, and seems best used when the kids ask to do "that music writing" again.

Hearing "Thais" by Massenet

Sorrow, mad feelings!
Loneliness, hurt feelings!
Lies caused this shameful thing!
Regrets are in their minds.
Families are being torn apart!
Mothers, and daughters crying out loud,
Tears spilling out of their eyes.
Loved ones being isolated.
A family they are no more!
They are no longer loved ones but
strangers.
A neighbor arrives.
That person thinks it is sad that the
family
Is no longer united.
What a friend!
He helps the family become reunited.
Thanks to the thoughtfulness of their
neighbor.
They are so happy!
That they cry with joy!
They are a family again.
Hugs and kisses come by the millions!
—**Christina Lee**

Collage!

Old newspapers are easy to come by. So are old magazines.

This activity uses them, and necessitates also that you have glue (or paste) and scissors.

If you don't have a class set of glue and scissors, a few sets will do. But in that case you'll have to make these activities separate, individual activities, done at a table in the back of the room while the rest of the class is engaged in something else.

The student goes through the newspaper looking for large or small headlines that might describe herself. They might be words—"Brilliant," "Colorful"—or they might be entire phrases or sentences: "Proves She Can Sail to Antartica," "The Longest Hair in Ecuador."

The student assembles many of these—does not glue them yet, but cuts out as many words or phrases as possible that describe herself. (Fantasy encouraged, too!)

Then, of course, on a piece of paper—large construction paper, if you have access to some—the words are glued on *in the order of the student's choice, and in the arrangement of the student's choice.* The point here is not linear poetry or prose such as one might encounter in a book; this activity is half art and half writing. So let the kids decide how this collage-of-self should go! (Don't forget—the possibilities kids can include are endless. They can cut out the names of foods they like, places they might like to visit, sports they like to play, and so forth.)

175

(Caution, though. The temptation is to let kids cut out pictures that appeal to them or describe them. No! We're working with *words* here; working with pictures is appropriate in other activities—not this one.)

Collage Variation #1: Found Poem

A found poem is any string of words you find that sounds poetic: poetic as in rhythmic, poetic as in crazy words together, poetic as in nonsensical but sounding good to the tongue, or poetic as in weird juxtapositions.

The activity: using the newspaper or magazine, the student goes through *quickly*, and cuts out anything that catches his eye—something that appeals to him in any way, no matter what the level. A phrase of a headline might be completely "gross"; a sentence in an article might make him hungry; half of a headline might just *sound* good.

Again, the student cuts out these attractive phrases or sentences. (Of course, single words are fine, too.)

Now, as you've guessed, he assembles the "finds" on his paper, and makes a poem of them. This time it is linear, and when it's glued, the form of a poem is seen.

A hint on this one. Sometimes what the student assembles in front of him—before gluing—doesn't seem at all satisfying to the student. The solution? More seeking, more cutting. Not everything has to be used, of course. Since the student is the sculptor of the poem, he's got every right to discard. (Maybe you can talk about the marble that great sculptors chip away and discard before their masterpieces take final shape!)

176

Collage Variation #2: Found Story

Same process, except whole paragraphs are lifted, mixed up, and changed here and there to make a story fall into place.

This activity is not recommended for classes with low frustration levels, but if you have classes with lots of tenacity and good senses of humor, I recommend trying this. Some crazy stories can result, and what's also of interest grammatically is the alteration that needs to be made before these stories hold together.

Poetry or Prose: Ugly!

Good writing is often neither kind nor unkind. It describes. The more accurately it describes, the better it is.

Not all things or people in our world are pleasant to behold. So: let the kids go. Ask them to describe, in poetry or prose, an ugly man or woman they conjure in their imagination. Not allowed: vulgar language. Remember—this exercise sharpens descriptive powers, so no copouts to the familiar foul words!

Kids *really* get into this activity. They'll try to outdo each other for the truly ugliest description. If you, as the teacher, circulate while they're writing, saying things like, "Oh, my goodness—Lisa's character is so disgusting!" the kids will take energy from that, and the derby is on.

Obviously, a ground rule is that no description can even remotely resemble a student or teacher (!) at school. Allowing this changes the energy of this activity, and is cruel.

The Man Was Ugly

The man was so ugly that he would make a witch beautiful. He smelled so dirty that you could plant a tree in his hair. When it rained, mud came down from his hair. When he spit on wood it ate the wood up. When he drank, he backwashed and whatever he was drinking turned green. He had so much wax in his ears you could make candles. He smelled like last year's milk.

—**Winston Foote**

CHAPTER FIVE

Letters to . . .
Letters from

Some of the most moving, gratifying writing I've seen has come from these activities.

The "letters" you encounter in this section are not "real" letters, though sometimes their poignancy is so *real life* that it's downright painful.

It is in activities like these that the previously mentioned idea of cultivating *compassion* can be shown. A student you once categorized as being "in his own world" will often, in letter-activities such as these, demonstrate a succinctness and power and sense of empathy that will take your breath away.

Again, in these activities, *openness* on the teacher's part is desirable. I've often begun an assignment from this group of ideas and had *the kids themselves* expand and open the possibilities.

An example: At the time that we as a class and the world as a whole were horrified at the June 1989 massacre of students in Tien'anmen Square in Beijing, I thought it appropriate to ask the kids to write a "Letter from a Student." I asked the kids to themselves *become* a student who was in the square that evening, and write a letter to the world

That's how it started. Soon kids began asking questions. "Can it be from a soldier?" "Can it be from a student's parents?" "Does the student have to be still alive?" On and on. Of course, all these were O.K.: their writers' interests were there—not necessarily in the idea I began with. At the end, when the letters were second and third draft done and handed in, I had letters from students, foreign reporters, parents, soldiers, young children, slain students, ghosts, tourists, a mother, and a doctor treating injured students. Beyond anything I would have imagined, and a very moving experience for me as a teacher.

How basic and beautiful letters are: messages from one to another.

Letter from a Soldier

This one may be a tear-jerker for you, and will be one that engages the kids.

Tell the kids that each one of them—girl and boy alike—is a soldier participating in a real war. Get them in the mood to write from this point of view: without moralizing, describe if you can the physical conditions of a combat soldier. Don't go too far, though, for too much description will either come back to you verbatim or will rob the kids of their own images.

Now tell the kids to write a letter home. The letter can be addressed to anyone they love. If they don't love anyone (say this, though you hope it not to be true), tell them to write to someone they know.

Encourage the kids to write using their five senses: what they see, feel, smell, taste, hear. Tell them to write in the letter how they are feeling, what they are thinking.

Some powerful works comes from this activity. It seems to work best in a quiet room, each student working singly.

Dear Jacky

Dear Jacky,

I know I haven't sent a letter to you for a while. The reason why is that the war is getting worse. I watched one of my friends get blown in half.

Whenever I think about it, I feel like running home and going AWOL.

Well sorry about boring you with stories. I'm doing pretty good. I hope you are doing the same.

I get out of this hell-hole in three months.

—**Joey Wilson**

Letter to Something
That Never Will Answer

It's a beautiful day! A day to take the kids outside!

This activity, with some classes, begins with some resistance, but wins hearts after all.

Get the kids outside. On the schoolyard bench, on the playing field, wherever it is possible for them to sit quietly and work.

Tell the kids that they are to write *a letter full of questions* to something outside that can never possibly answer their letter, except, perhaps, in dreams.

Write to the wind. ("Where do you come from? Wind, what have you carried?") Write to a garbage can, to flies, to grass, to ants, to a hubcap in the road . . . a million possibilities.

It's possible to learn about students by noticing what those students choose to write. Results from this activity are often very good, and kids enjoy it.

Embarrassment and confidentiality get in the way of peer proofreading of letters, so a second draft process might be best done individually here.

Letter from the Dead

Eerie as this may seem, it results in good work.

Ask the kids to think of a dead person: perhaps a distant historical figure, perhaps a modern-day figure, perhaps someone in their family, perhaps a friend.

Have the kids put their heads down. The class is quiet, and you, while the kids are relaxing, ask them (1) to picture that person in their minds, (2) to imagine that person writing a letter (to them, to the class, to the entire world, whatever), and (3) to imagine some of the things that person might like to say.

When you're ready, have the kids sit up and quietly begin to write. This is a *no-talking* exercise, requiring not only meditation, but also privacy.

When the letters are finished, some kids may want to volunteer to read their letters. Others will not want to, and should be respected. Do try to read them all, however, as a teacher. Some profound work can come of this. Don't be disappointed if this activity doesn't come off; it either works well or includes too much sarcasm and silliness. (Which is not to say that good humor-work can't come from this; it can if not epidemic in the class.)

A Basketball Star's Final Letter

Several months ago, Hank Gathers, a basketball superstar for the Loyola Marymount team, died while he was playing

in a playoff game. Heart problems led
him to this fate.

I am living peacefully and am watching television in my home. Later, I go
outside to get the mail from the mailbox,
not knowing what I am about to get.
There in my hand, I hold a letter that is
addressed to me and is from, shockingly,
Hank Gathers! At first, I think I am
dreaming, so I try to lose that dream, but
later I find that it is true!

After I finally come to grips with
what is happening, I go back to my bed
and sit there, opening the letter. Then I
take out the sheet of paper and read
what is on it.

*Hey, Kenneth, I know you're probably
shocked at this, but I had to tell you
something. You saw me collapse at that
playoff game, didn't you? Well, that was
because I did not take my doctor's advice
and left my medicine. I wanted to play
the game and thought that "just some
medicine" I did not take wouldn't hurt
me much. I also wanted to tell you that
if I did not make that mistake and play
so hard that my heart couldn't control
my body, I would still be living today.
So remember not to overwork when
you're doing your work or anything else,
like playing sports, etc.*

Suddenly the letter disappeared and I felt strange at what I had just faced. So I fell on my bed and went to sleep. The next day, I woke up confused at what had happened the day before, but I still clearly remembered something. I forgot how I got it in my head, but I knew someone had told me:

Not to overwork when you're doing your work or anything else. . . . It still lingers in my mind today.

—**Kenneth Jew**

Letter to the Dead

By the time a child reaches middle school, she or he usually has had someone important die. This person may be a grandparent. Too often it is a parent, a sibling, or a friend.

This activity should be approached with the utmost sensitivity. If you don't have control of your class, don't try it. Privacy should be paramount, and each child's dignity should be given room.

Introduce the activity by saying something like, "Most of us have had someone dear to us die. Maybe a grandparent, an aunt or an uncle, maybe even a parent or a brother or sister, or a good friend. It can be a bad feeling for us . . . maybe for some people there's a little bit of good feeling mixed in. And most of us have thought of things we'd like to say to that person, but we can't say anything, because they're dead. . . ."

Continue now to suggest that the kids focus on one important, dead person to whom they'd like to say something. Ask the kids to put their writing in the form of a letter. Of course the letter has no actual destination, and you might want to say that just for the saying of it.

Now emphasize the *total* privacy of this activity. This is a letter that you as a teacher will not read, and will not ask to read. This is a letter to be shown only if the student wants to show it. Use your own judgment on this; it seems that some kids' desire to please the teacher could move you into the realm of impropriety and a confidentiality you might not be able to reciprocate correctly.

This activity is a strong one, and the mood of the classroom will impress you.

Letter to a Classmate

This one takes some finesse to pull off properly, but its results can be gratifying.

Have each student put his or her name on a small piece of paper and crumple the paper. Take a container around the room and collect the papers.

Tell the students ahead of time, "You're going to be writing a letter to someone in the class you don't know very well. You'll be asking this person questions about himself or herself.

The kids will complain like crazy. As you exchange names (either randomly or by assignment, randomly seeming better); you intervene to make sure that (1) good friends don't get together, (2) boys and girls mix, and (3) no slurs—racial, personal, or whatever—occur. The latter is good to warn about ahead of time.

Once the kids get to work on this, they actually enjoy it, and it's really good for classroom esprit-de-corps! Things to discourage in this are satire, sarcastic questions, and sexual explicitness or innuendo.

Letter from a Literary Character

The class is reading a book. Or has just read a book—preferably a good novel, but a biography or autobiography would be fine, too.

Have the kids write a letter from a character of their—or, if necessary, of your—choice.

The letter might explain that character's actions and be addressed to the class, or to the "reader." Or the letter might be addressed to another character in the book. In the latter case the letter might be one of apology, one of threat, one of love, explanation, entreaty, . . .

This activity helps deepen particular characters in the minds of kids, and, if the letters are discussed in class, can help kids understand the dynamic process involved in creating a character and that character's conflicts and resolutions.

CHAPTER SIX

Monologues/ Dialogues

One-Sided Conversation: Telephone or Otherwise

There is a wonderful piece by Jean Cocteau entitled, "The Human Voice." In it, there is only one speaker, and that speaker is a woman speaking on the telephone to a lover who has jilted her.

Playing a tape of this, if possible, is a wonderful way to begin this activity, but it is not necessary.

Have the kids write conversation overheard from one end of the telephone. Emphasize the idea that people don't always converse in complete sentences; they use slang, they interrupt and are interrupted. Ask the kids to make sure the reader/listener can guess what the *story* or *situation* is between the two people. What is being said from the other side? What kind of person is on the other end of this connection? Emphasize reality (whatever that is) and, most of all, *realistic patterns of speech.*

You'll get some good response from this one (teen-age pregnancy, plots to rob liquor stores . . .) and kids enjoy reading their work to the class. (Don't forget that in this particular performance the *pause* has at least as much power as the spoken line.)

Of course one-sided conversations needn't be restricted to the telephone, but in this activity, telephones, being the mechanical instruments most used by kids, seem to work best.

Variation: One-Sided Conversation

Have the kids write their own "first side," pair up
with other kids, switch papers, and write responses to the
"first sides." They love it. (Good to discuss profanity here:
O.K. if completely in context of the situation—and realistic;
not O.K. if used for its own sake, or for the sake of getting
guffaws out of fellow classmates in a reading . . .)

The Obscene Call

RRRRRRRRNG!

Hello?
Hello?
Is anyone there?
Listen bud, do you have a
breathing problem or what?
What am I wearing?
That's disgusting!
What?
No I'm not naked!!
Who is this?
Stop that breathing!
Don't you have anything
better to do?
What?
Well I never!
Listen, I happen to be happily
married!
Oh yeah, well hold on!
Honey!

Hello?

Beeeeeeeeep_____!

—Lily Bendo

One-Sided Conversation: Fill in the Missing Voice

Though not as completely "creative" as other activities in this book, this idea is fun, and I've had good results with it.

I write one side of a dialogue on the board. It's the kids' job—individually—to write the other side. You'll be amazed at the differences in the responses you'll get.

A sample of what I write: use it if it fits, but you'll probably have more fun devising your own.

> *Hello?*
> *Yes, it is.*
> *When?*
> *After work.*
> *Had dinner.*
> *My wife and kids.*
> *Thursday.*
> *He did?*
> *Oh, my God!*
> *When?*
> *Of course!*
> *Tonight?*
> *If you insist.*

195

Keep it short—more interpretation is available in such brevity.

Dramatic Monologue

This can take the form of prose, poetry, or drama drawn in lines.

Ask the kids to imagine that they are someone else—a historical figure, a close relative, a teacher, an unnamed old man, any human.

Let the kids think for awhile, then ask them to write down what that person wants to tell us. (Use first-person voice.)

The kids will come up with stories, poems, etc.

For kids who get stuck, get them to have the character ask questions and answer them herself.

For kids who seem to have a knack for a good dramatic line, encourage them to write the monologue line by line in true-to-life speech.

Do be prepared to offer a wide spectrum of possible "subjects" when kids begin this activity. Let them know that ones they themselves choose are much better than yours, and that you are only offering these names as a way to break the ice.

Dialogues with the Imaginary

This should entail the making of a two-part dialogue. One part is that of the student, and the other part is a character of the student's imagination.

The character might be the President of the Universe, a horse, the sun, a dust speck that comes alive, a cavewoman, a dinosaur, Halley's comet—anything of the student's imagining.

The emphasis here is that no narration (a little intro might be O.K.) or description is allowed. Straight dialogue.

Dialogues with the "Real"

Same as above, except the student chooses a living person with whom to speak. That person might be the student's father, the school principal, an enemy, a girlfriend/boyfriend, an undersea explorer, or whatever persona the student comes up with.

Again, no narrative or exposition. Dialogue must be depended on for dramatic effect! Let the words do the moving, the description—all of it!

CHAPTER SEVEN

Artwork: Possibilities Wide & Deep

Y ou walk into an art museum. There is a special exhibition on. You wander through, intrigued by one painting, nonplussed by another, completely baffled by another, and then it happens: a particular painting strikes you so deeply you stand transfixed in front of it for ten minutes, then move to the bench in the middle of the room so that you can sit and be drawn into the painting, have its colors envelop you, its figures enter your life . . .

I think most of us have had this experience, or a variation of it. The form might be sculpture or it might be photography. The place it occurs might be in a museum or in a library while looking at a book of twentieth-century photographs. Or the place might be an exhibition of masks from Africa or a flea market where one encounters a box of old lithographs. Wherever it occurs, we know that we have been touched deeply, and we are grateful.

Each of us brings the whole body of our experience into our relationship with a given work of art. Almost ritualistically, we stand before it and offer ourselves, and the art object offers itself, and there is a reciprocity, a mutual giving and taking. No two people, it seems, could possibly have the same thoughts and feelings about a particular painting or sculpture or photograph or artifact. Two of us might say we *love it* or *are confused by it*, but the precise words we might use and the particular wellspring of feeling informing our reactions would not ever be the same.

It is for this reason that there are unbelievably broad possibilities to be found in kids writing face-to-face with art. Given an adequate range of works, lovely and expressive writing can come from the use of art as an entrée in emotion and imagination of students. In the same way that poetry is a very direct and nonjudgmental way to open doors of easy writing for kids, so too is a picture on a page or sculpture on a pedestal or a gruesome mask on a wall. Kids don't need to "know" anything to *be let in*, here; they simply need to feel and think. How rich and renewable is this resource!

Truly, a skilled (and energetic!) teacher could do an entire year focused on art-writing without kids being bored (or boring themselves) once!

What follows are just a few activities that mine this deep vein. I might mention that in my own experience, basically functioning groups tend to respond better to art that is very representational, whereas higher level groups seem capable of responding to work that might occasionally be less representational, less figurative, and more abstract. However, I may have been going about things all wrong these years; and you may find that basic-level groups do better writing with work that is very abstract. Give it a try.

A Story in There, a Life in There

The ideal here is that there are as many reproductions of good art (use the Masters) as there are kids in the class. Reproductions might be posted, made available for student choice, or available in books. You might have five each of six different reproductions or, better, thirty different prints.

The teacher stands before the class and holds up a reproduction of a painting (drawing, etc.) which particularly strikes her heart. Figurative work seems better, though abstract *can* be used.

The teacher talks about the artist, talks of how when an artist begins a painting, that artist is *lost* inside that painting, a willing surrender to the characters and the environment she or he is creating. The painting may (or may not) show a moment in a life, a moment in a dramatic story, or other moments.

Now ask the kids to choose a reproduction that particularly strikes their *hearts*. Tell them not to think about it, just go to it the way iron goes to a magnet.

When they have done that, tell them to lose themselves inside the painting: completely leave the classroom, put their entire *selves* in the milieu of the work, dive in!

Now, ask them to write in the voice of a character or object in the painting. What is the person thinking? Why? What is the situation? What is the future? Let the figure in the painting speak. An object, as well, can speak: an old tire in a junk yard, a ship sinking in a towering sea, many possibilities.

Variation #1: Artworks

If there are more figures in the art piece, ask the student to speak in the voice of each figure. Emphasize differences of voice.

This works only if kids are good at individual motivation or if all kids have a reproduction with a number of figures in it. If this situation does not exist, encourage kids with, say, a single figure in their painting, to *continue* and write from the perspective of the chair, the violin, the bird in the tree, or others.

Variation #2: Self-Artworks

In this activity, kids do their own art, paint their own painting, draw their own drawings, then, when done, speak (in writing!) from the voice of someone/thing in their creation. (See another variation of this activity in the discussion of kid-created fables and tales.)

Incidentally, the artwork in this activity need not be done at school. You can simply assign kids the homework of picture creation, and ask them to bring the work to school. (Who among us can spontaneously do creative work with thirty other people crowded around us! How admirable kids are to be able to produce *anything* of creative worth in the classroom!)

Variation #3: Poetry in Art

Art lends itself to poetry as well as, if not better than, to prose.

Kids can focus on (lose themselves in) a picture and begin a poem on *anything* contained therein. Let the poem be in someone's voice, or not. Let the poem begin with one word of description, add words, describe feelings, catalogue violence both obvious and subtle, speak in the voice of the painter himself, rant and rave about life, paint with random words, *anything*.

The point in all this is that the poem should do what good art does: evoke from us an emotion, a thought, a general or specific response in a way that is important to us as individuals.

Variation #4: Writing to Photographs

There are, of course, many ways to do this. You might have a collection of pictures to pass around, you might get books of photo collections of the Masters (landscapes work less well than portraits), or you might provide for the kids magazines that contain high-quality people-photos. *National Geographic* is quite good for this purpose; you can always find a good number of used copies; photo quality is good, and subject matter is exotic. Whatever you use, don't use junk: grocery newsstand copies featuring photos of current stars, etc. Let the kids' responses be original.

The activity is virtually the same as those using reproductions of fine art. Ask the kids either to: (1) in a narrative, *tell the story of the man in the straw hat pull-ing the donkey up the steep precipice,* or (2) *actually speak in the voice of the man.*

The activity can be extended, again, by asking the students to either tell the *whole* story (past, present, maybe future) or by speaking from the voice of *all* the characters represented in the photo or collection.

There are so many resources for this activity! Use them! Oh Ben Franklin! Oh Free Libraries!

Don't forget poetry here! It doesn't bite!

On "Dancer on the Stage"
by Edgar Degas

As the vast and decorative curtains open to reveal and display the elegant scenery of the stage, it is my opportunity to dance for the lovely audience. Attired in an exquisite ballet outfit with white tutu, tights, and a pair of white satin ballet slippers. I run and leap like a tender yet vivacious fawn, who, for the first time, is able to play and frolic with its animal friends. My meager yet strong feet guide me to my stationed place. Nervousness hovers upon me but is instantly eradicated when the concentrated music I know so well is played.

Then, as by mystical sorcery, the hypnotic music covers my outer shell of existence with an indestructible aura which only I know. So therefore, my arms, feet, and body are compelled to endure these articulate yet delicate maneuvers.

I leap, split, pivot, pirouette, and accomplish other spectacular ballet steps with the same characteristics of grace and agility as the mighty and majestic bald eagle possesses. Considering this is my debut, I must confess that I was past the stage of excellence, maybe even superb! I should know, because discharging a dazzling smile and a thumbs up of success are my dance instructor, attired in a black tuxedo, and my fellow colleagues of dancing.

My dress, bright, clean, and decorated with satin and flowers, sparkles while my sash waves frantically to the audience. I'm lost in a magical dimension where I am the wind entertaining only the people who are observing me like numerous fluorescent stars up in the sky and atmosphere. Then bang! The sweet array of beautiful sounds from the prominent orchestra concludes with a thundering roar. Clapping, and cherished bravos cram my head until I bow and leave the stage in an exuberant but graceful manner to face more congratulations. Embedded within my soul is the perception that this is the beginning of a very promising and successful career.

—**Theresa Pulanco**

CHAPTER EIGHT

How to Produce
a School
Literary Magazine

People

People—who are they?
Are they real?
Do they really love?
Where do they come from?
How did they become?
I mean the first of them?
In which way do you see them?
Do you really know them?
Are you hiding from them?
I mean are you being yourself?
Who are they?
They are the ones we call . . . people.

—Tanya Brown

In a school, a literary magazine can be an extremely open activity.

The scope of its involvement can be determined precisely by the adult or adults who guide it. The magazine project can be built to involve just a few kids, a single class, a group (gifted, ethnic, etc.) — or, more inclusively, it can be designed to involve a deep and wide variety of students in a school's population.

Elementary kids can do it. Middle schoolers can do it; high schoolers can do it.

A literary magazine can be small, informally produced, and come out a few times per year, or, at the other end of possibilities, can be large, professionally produced, and issued only once a year.

According to the wishes of its adult guide, the department from which it springs, or its student staff, it might be very specific in its internal scope, or as broad as the possibilities inherent in student writing. It might contain poetry only, prose only, student drama, or an admixture of these.

It might or might not include drawings or other reproducible student art.

The more wide-ranging, inclusive, and varied it is, the more faculty and student support is necessary, if only on a basic level. The smaller in scope the magazine is, conversely, the fewer individuals need to be involved and, ultimately, will be involved in a final product.

What immediately follows here is an extremely biased discussion of how I believe a school literary magazine should be done. Then, for those choosing either to concur with these biases or to disagree with them, there is a step-by-step sequence of how actually to produce a literary magazine of the quality of your choice.

I think that a school-sponsored magazine should include the maximum number of students possible. After all, aren't the ideas of maximum involvement, process, and pride in a product well wrought by serious labor some of the concepts we as educators want our kids to get?

Maximum involvement entails some "advertising." This might include classroom-to-classroom hustling on the part of either the faculty coordinator or last year's staff members, announcement in school bulletins, proselytizing by English teachers, word of mouth, or a combination of these.

Once two thousand (fifty?) kids show up for the initial meeting, you've got to be prepared to give them something to do. I'll detail possible committees in the "How To" section, but would like to mention that this initial meeting will reinforce for you both a success and a challenge: kids of all levels show up for this meeting. You know that not all of them are capable either of publishing fine work or of editing such, so:

- This is why I think that black-and-white drawings are a great outlet, in part for kids who might have difficulty writing.
- This is why *some* committees ought to be set up that by nature are non-academic.

Other biases come into play. I mention them briefly.

The nature of a literary magazine is one that is not an organ of school propaganda, messages from authorities, deadly essays on Christopher Columbus, or wimpy prize-winning essays on "Why I Think Math Is Important." It's a place where writing by kids can be enjoyed by kids. If, as a by-product, adults enjoy the work, too, more joy to both parties.

All kinds of poetry, fiction, drama, and experimental writing should be fair game for the magazine. Essays should be considered if they're engaging on a level other than their adherence to a teacher's dogma, their grammaticality, or their mere predictability.

Poetry should be varied. Some rhyme is O.K.—kids do like to rhyme—but rhyme should not be the prescribed or encouraged form. Rhyme binds the writing of kids—and adults, too, for that matter—and constricts the level of expression. Short poems, long ones, prosy ones, sexy ones, grief-stricken ones, questioning ones, strange ones—all should be welcomed!

Spelling in prose and poetry should be corrected. This avoids postpublication embarrassment to the writer.

Grammar, however, should be tampered with as little as possible. Does the erroneous grammar obstruct our way to sense? If so, fix it. Will the constructions of, for example, an English-as-a-second-language student later subject her or him to mockery? Fix them. Too often, though, fresh ways of saying things or rhythmic ways of sending words to the reader are excised by the skilled surgery of a teacher's red pen, and words that one *lived* are now relegated to the dung-heap of lifeless phrases.

Speaking of dung, what about rough language, scatalogical reference, super-graphic violence, or sexual innuendo and explicitness? A good rule would go something like this: with the terrible specter of Censorship at your back, use a balance scale. In one pan, place the high student-reader interest these words are sure to elicit. In the other pan, place the work. Is it good writing? Does it perhaps describe a kid-expression or a kid-condition not much written about? Or is it written strictly for reaction, with no deeper redeeming value at all? You decide, but err if you must on the side of expression written by real kids.

By this last paragraph I'd not want to imply that the work coming your way will be raw or tawdry. To be sure, some of it will, but the great bulk of it will carry a great dignity, and some of it will be absolutely transcendent.

Regarding power (here, editorial power), do try to give as much of it as possible to the kids. Let kids make a majority of editorial decisions, while at the same time reserving some discretion for yourself as faculty coordinator. The "How To" discusses ways I've found to be successful in this. The point here is that the less students feel they're minions, the more they'll think of the magazine as theirs, and the more returnees/new recruits you'll get next year!

Finally, the product. If you have the money, or if you can get the money, make it handsome and do it right. A real book—perfect-bound in the manner of a paperback— need not be too expensive, and can last a lifetime. Some students may never publish again or see their artwork in any other public place. They'll keep the magazine a lifetime. Remember that trophy you got (or didn't get) when you were a kid? Make it a trophy.

The Power

I sat there with my hands reaching out. And in front of me stood a line of thousands of people, young and old, waiting for me to touch them. I sat on this very same chair ten hours every day touching thousands of people. Why? Because I had the power to cure all pains, diseases, and even sadness. I had the healing hands. I could make people feel happy when I touched them. I could cure any kind of pain and disease. I had this strange power in my hands. My hands were a gift to society, but a burden to myself.

You might think that I should be very happy to have had such power. But you're wrong. I cannot feel with my hands. It is like I am wearing a pair of gloves.

Everything I touch feels the same. The coldness, warmness, and softness of all things I can not feel. I don't even feel pain when I cut myself.

My hands were dead when I was born. They were borrowed to serve others. But what about me? I was depressed and my mind drove me crazy. I was tired of being used as a machine. Some nuts thought I was the devil and tried to kill me several times. This world is unfair, unfair to me. Now that I am old, my healing power is no longer with me. I am not needed anymore. I am a waste. I want to die.

—**Minh Thai**

At Last: The How-To

Steps to Producing a School Literary Magazine

1. Decide at the outset not only what kind of magazine you'd like to make (see previous page), but what its physical attributes will be. What you want the product to be will largely determine needs—number of pages, how much work should be included or excluded, and the number of copies to be made.

The following are formats of a literary magazine, listed in ascending order of quality:

- Dittoed, folded, and stapled at school.
- Dittoed, covered with thicker paper, folded, and stapled professionally. (A copy shop can fold and staple for a small fee.)
- Mimeographed, folded, and stapled at school. (Mimeo allows for more copies than ditto; illustration, however, is trickier to include unless you have a stencil scanner.)
- Mimeographed, covered with thicker paper, then folded and stapled professionally.
- Photocopied well, folded, and stapled at school.
- Photocopied well and covered with thicker paper at school, folded and stapled professionally.
- Offset printed, covered, folded, and stapled professionally. This product is

a relatively inexpensive option used by a number of small national literary magazines.

- Offset printed on plain white or colored paper, covered with a thick glossy black-and-white cover, and perfect-bound, like a paperback book.
- Offset printed on white or colored paper, covered with a thick glossy one-or-two-color cover, and perfect bound.
- Letterpress printed on fancy paper—colored or white—covered with thick stock, perfect-bound or sewn professionally, and using many different-colored inks.

It should be noted that a multicolored, glossy format for the entire book would be prohibitively expensive for the great majority of public schools. Endowed private schools might well afford such an extravagance.

Folding is, of course, not necessary. An 8½ × 11 inch magazine can be done somewhat more easily. It also looks less like a book, if that factor is one you want to consider.

In the case of *offset printing*, it usually is possible to choose a specific color of ink for the printing of the text. If any extra charge is involved, that usually is slight.

Photographs are possible to include in a literary magazine, but if a high-quality reproduction is what you want, something called a "half-tone stat" should first be made. The stat costs extra money and often is available from the printer. If not, a business that specializes in graphic production can help you.

Regarding *drawings*, it is greatly preferable that all drawings be submitted in black pen on white paper. Other inks or papers don't reproduce as well as these.

Of course, other media besides line drawings also work well. Woodcuts, lino-prints, computer art, Chinese/Japanese traditional drawings or paintings, black-and-white collages, or architectural designs all work well if contrast is high enough for good resolution in the offset process. Experiment on a photocopying machine if you're not sure how a given artwork might reproduce.

Finally, do try to include at least one work from each student who submits art. Kids' feelings are important, and transcend highfalutin adult aesthetic doctrine. Remember that even small drawings, pasted up felicitously beside short poems or works of prose, can make a big difference in magazine appearance!

2. Call a meeting of interested students. See how many you get. Look 'em over, and, if you know the kids, mentally assess their skill levels.

3. Explain to the kids what the project is about. Show examples, if possible. Emphasize *fun* and the joy of recognizing and publishing good writing!

4. Depending on the number of kids, decide how many committees you need. Many kids = wide skill level = many committees. Here are some possible committees:

Editors	Proofreaders	Illustrators
Typists	Graphics workers	Paste-up
Production	Word processors	Distribution

Allow students to sign up for more than one com mittee if they so desire. A vital core of good and interested workers will emerge.

From the first meeting to the end of the project, figure a 10 to 20 percent dropout rate.

Assure kids on the later-acting committees (paste-up, distribution, etc.) that they *will* play an important part!

Important note: At this meeting, be ready to distribute white paper and black pens to prospective illustrators. Some kids can't afford pens of their own, and others aren't well organized enough to buy the material. It's worth the investment. I tell the kids that I want the pens back later, but I never ask for them back. Also, I hand out 5 × 7 white *cards* instead of paper. They're durable, and kids are kids.

Two important things should be stressed to the illustrators. The first is the concept of *originality*. Many kids don't really understand what it means to be original. I emphasize imagination, emphasize work coming from their heads and hearts, and *not* copied from a comic strip, magazine illustration, toy carton, etc. Any work that is derivative (directly) will be admired, but not considered. Second, give the illustrators a *deadline* today. Let it be a good amount of time—at least a month—and, during that time, try to encourage your illustrators as you pass them in the hall, see them in the yard, or greet them in class.

5. Set the date for the next meeting. Try to have meetings at the same time each week, so that kids can put aside that time. The next meeting should be for editors and proofreaders, but it seems a good policy to invite anyone on the staff who'd like to sit in and listen

Now, start gathering work to read at the next meeting. Encourage kids to submit *any* writing; cajole colleagues into saving decent work, spirited work; do specific writing projects with your classes; sponsor little competitions; *anything* (almost) to get submissions

6. *Now* we're at your next meeting. Your editors (there might be twenty of them!) and proofreaders are there. You have a sheaf of papers to be considered.

Here's the way I approach the process, though you may want to vary it according to the sophistication of your kids:

The teacher sits in a central place. She or he assigns a secretary who, for every work accepted, fills the "Work Accepted" form (see attached) noting the title of the piece, the author, and the first line.

The teacher (or adult) then reads each still-anonymous work orally, giving it as fine a reading as she or he can. Without directly trying to influence the kid-editors' choice, this is a great place to teach! You can talk about rhythm, realism, flow, many positive things. There's no need to get into negative criticism: the kids will do enough of that themselves.

After reading each work, simply take a vote. Cruel as it seems, I do a simple "thumbs up/thumbs down" majority vote. My vote doesn't count, and I try to let my feelings remain unshown.

However, I do on occasion "channel" things. If a good piece of work is voted down, I show concern and try to determine why. When the *why* of their rejection becomes apparent (and often it's cloudy), I do my best to try quickly teaching the concept of just where the piece is powerful or lovely. Then I'll read it again, and ask for another vote. If the kids still say no, I respect that.

However again, I do reserve myself ten vetoes on writing and five on acceptance of drawings. It seems quite important that striking or powerful work submitted in good faith *not* be rejected. This "veto" count becomes a fine game with the staff, and do they ever keep track!

So: every time you have work accepted, pass the work to the day's secretary. He or she will log in the afore-mentioned information. Then you'll take the work and put it in a folder of submissions accepted. After each meeting, this accepted work is passed along to the typing or word-processing (God, what a phrase) committee. It really helps to have the cooperation of the school typing or word-processing teacher in this. Our wonderful typing teacher has been critical to our magazine, and one year, when no accurate typists were available from student ranks, she actually typed the entire manuscript herself—above and beyond the call of duty.

Note on Typing: If you are typing the manuscript, and if it is possible, use a high-quality typewriter with a good, clear typeface and a new ribbon. Your magazine will look much better. These days we're using a word processor—a Macintosh, in this case—and are ecstatic about the results. With a laser printer, you can get a look that is close to typesetting, yet the process is easy enough that a student can do it. You can choose among a dozen or so type fonts, you can vary the size of the type, make italics and bold-lettered titles or headlines. Fantastic. If there isn't a laser printer at school, there must be one somewhere around town. They're worth seeking out, and look so much better than that sterile and uniform dot-matrix computer printer look! (*Caution:* make sure your computer disk is set up for laser printing!)

Note on Acceptance/Rejection of Work: Obviously, it is better to accept all work, but that is not always possible. Since most student submissions come from teachers, those rejected don't even need to know this has occurred; their teacher simply receives back the paper unmarked. those accepted usually don't know until the magazine is published. This, it seems, absolutely minimizes bad feelings or jealousy.

Final Note on the Editorial Process: Of course, all work considered is read anonymously—no name, no grade, no hints. Only after acceptance of a work does the adult guide announce the name of the student writer. Any work rejected is kept anonymous, unless of course that rejection is vetoed by the adult.

7. These meetings continue to occur until you have enough writing to fill your magazine. Don't forget to leave pages open for illustrations, title page, acknowledgments, staff lists, etc.

8. After all writing is accepted (and, it is hoped, typed or word-processed by now) call in your illustrations.

Have a meeting where illustrations are chosen. I try to encourage votes not only for high-quality drawing, but also for work that is different, spirited, iconoclastic, dignified, or otherwise significant.

9. You have your writing. You have your illustrations. You are now ready to go into your *production* phase. Call a meeting of the graphics crew. These people will make the titles and authors' names in the manner you've chosen. There are at least five ways to go on this:

- You simply have typed the titles and authors. In that case, step 9 is unnecessary.
- You can identify kids who are good calligraphers to do the titles and names of authors. Try for the same hand on each, though, and experiment with a uniform size.
- You can purchase rub-down type at an art supply store. This type comes on large sheets with many of each letter and number. The variety available is amazing. Kids transfer the type with a pencil or burnishing tool (kind of like scratching away at a lottery ticket, only opposite) and the type appears on paper. Kids love to do this, but *caveat:* this process is extremely time-consuming and exacting. You've got to have a great crew to pull this one off!
- You can rent or borrow a wonderful machine called a Kroy-type. This machine uses wheels of various types

and a ribbon, and is operated somewhat like a typewriter. It is fast, kids get a charge out of using it, and the quality is quite acceptably high. Watch for smudges and stray black marks.

- You can use a word-processing program that allows you to vary typeface and size. It is possible, using something like the Macintosh, to do all of your graphics and typing at the same time—and have a very professional look, if you use a laser printer. The negative part of this sort of "modernization" is just what it is worldwide—the loss of jobs. Fewer kids get involved in the making of titles, authors' names, and final paste-up if you use a computer. Think about this when considering what your needs are.

10. Quite a few meetings will be needed to accomplish the graphics phase of production. Don't forget to have students do the cover title for the magazine and any other graphics necessary to the finished product. Do *proofread* all work—typing and graphics as well. How horrible to have writing published under a misspelled name!

11. Call a meeting of your paste-up crew. Supply them with: scissors (or, for a more advanced group, X-acto knives, available in art supply stores), glue sticks, typed text titles and authors. Post the "Work Accepted" lists on the wall.

Provide the kids with half-sheets of nonreproducible blue-inked graph paper with quarter-inch squares.

These, too, are available in art supply stores. Make sure the sheets, if cut, are cut professionally. Again, a copy shop will do this for you for a slight fee.

Now, have the kids *carefully* paste up the poems, stories, or other work. Emphasize following the straight blue lines of the graph paper, centering the cut-out titles, and putting authors names in an appropriate and consistent position.

Carefully monitor this paste-up process. It's what the magazine finally will look like!

Obviously, if you've used a word processor with a publishing program, this paste-up step will be greatly diminished in elaboration. Perhaps only the drawings will need to be pasted up.

12. This step is important. Quietly sit down with three or four careful, literate kids from your crew. Go over every pasted-up page for typos, crookedness, "lost" ends of stories, erroneous titles or author names, etc. Since this is a student publication, some mistakes will slip through the cracks, but do your best.

13. Meet with your paste-up and graphics crew, lay out all the pages on a huge table, and let students choose which pages should be first, which drawings should oppose which stories or poems, etc. Guide the process, making suggestions all the while. This part is fun! The magazine really is close to happening! To help you in this process, get a paperback book and follow the paperback book page by page as you decide on your page order. This helps you know which pages will oppose which, and will enable students to lightly blue-pencil in page numbers.

Once these penciled numbers are on the pages, put the work away and step away from the project for a few days. Get some space between you and the book.

After a few days, come back and look afresh. Make certain that your pages are where you want them, in the order that you want. Again, use a paperback book as your guide—it really helps.

O.K.? So put the page numbers on, using either press-down (rub-on) type or a typewriter. Try to do a good job on this, making the page number placement consistent.

14. Determine what kind of front cover you want. Determine what kind of back cover you want. What drawings should be there? What words will be printed? Where shall the magazine's name go? Decide these things. Have the graphics and paste-up crews do these things.

15. At this point, *congratulations!* You're almost ready to go to the printer. But: *stop!* take just one more day, collar a careful student, and ask him or her to put opaquing fluid on any surfaces that may have been smudged. There will be plenty of these, and you'll be glad you took this step.

16. Onward to the printer! By now you've researched the least expensive printers in town, struck a deal with one, reserved a date well before the end of school, and arrive on the agreed-on date with the work in your hand. Precious, precious work.

17. Two weeks or so later, you go get your books.

18. Your distribution committee goes into gear now. The books arrive at school. A good goal for distribution seems to be this: one free copy for every writer, one for each illustrator (two if a student has done both), one for every adult staff member, and a reasonable number for you to distribute to interested parties, both student and adult. The ideal? One for every kid in the school.

19. You did it!

20. The kids have put in a tremendous effort. They've produced a literary magazine that both looks good and reads well. Reward them with a field trip to a place of their choice. Of course, money constraints come into play here, but do what you can . . . they deserve it.

Me, the Ox

I feel huge, but cannot make a sound.
I feel tired, but cannot act it out.
I feel lonely, but nobody understands.
But someday I shall bellow so loud
I will be heard all over.
That's the day I will be known and
    understood.
                                    —Wendel Tse

"Work Accepted" Form

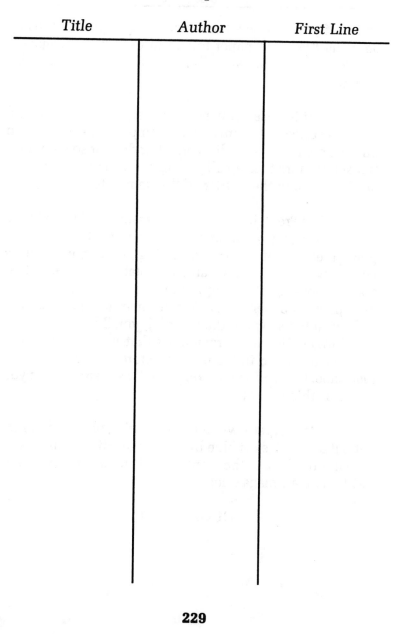

Title	Author	First Line

Typing

If you choose a book-style format, you'll probably be using 8½ × 11 paper folded in half. If the magazine is to be printed professionally, the printer will use this size paper.

In this case, you need to vary your typing and margins strategy. I simply draw a template of a 5 × 7 card on a ditto master, then ditto off a hundred or so copies for typists. Be sure to keep all typing and illustration at least 3/8 inch inside the border of this template.

If you're using a word processor, you'll be able to vary your margins automatically, and won't need a template. Ideally, your word-processing program will have a feature whereby you'll be able to "rotate" the page so that you're "looking at" and typing on the short side of a standard piece of paper. If you fix your margins right (be sure to leave a big space in the middle), you'll be close to the true format. However, remember that you'll have to cut these pages down in the middle before you assemble the magazine. (This all will become readily apparent when you arrive at this stage.)

Don't forget—when you're pasting up typed pages, cut out all vestiges of blue lines from the ditto. Otherwise, they'll reproduce at the printer. A clean original is essential to a clean magazine!

GOOD LUCK!

Selected Bibliography

Any bibliography on the teaching of writing must begin with an exhortation to mail away for the catalogue of the Teachers & Writers Collaborative, 5 Union Square West, New York, NY 10003. This catalogue lists some fifty excellent books on writing and the teaching of it, all based experientially—not simply philosophically.

Some particular recommendations from that catalogue:

The Whole Word Catalogue #2, edited by Bill Zavatsky and Ron Padgett. It's not necessary to have #1 to use this book well. It includes essays on theory, many activities, projects, and a good annotated bibliography. Highly recommended.

The Whole Word Catalogue #1, edited by Rosellen Brown, Marvin Hoffman, Martin Kushner, Phillip Lopate, and Sheila Murphy. A much shorter book than #2, but still good. Lots of activities for elementary kids included with the usual upper-grade suggestions.

Wishes, Lies, and Dreams, by Kenneth Koch. This is a still-current classic which broke open the teaching of creative writing in public schools. It's written by a poet and is informed by a fundamentally poetic sensibility. There are many good activities here for kids, and the *why* of them is exciting for teachers. Also recommended are Koch's *Rose, where did you get that red?* (Teaching Great Poetry to Children) and his *Sleeping on the Wing*, in collaboration with Kate Farrell. The latter is best for high school classes and not only presents interesting and accessible great poetry for reading, but also provides good activities springing from such poems.

The Writing Workshop, Volumes 1 and 2, by Alan Ziegler. I haven't yet seen Volume 2, but I love Volume 1. It is an in-depth, *open* discussion of the why's and how's of running a writing class, and ranges from nitty-gritty how-to suggestions to experienced discussions on ideas like line breaks in poetry. Lovely, caring, and written from a wise and humanistic sensibility.

Other works:

Getting from Here to There: Reading and Writing Poetry, by Florence Grossman, Heinemann Publishers, Portsmouth, New Hampshire. This is a good book whose author leads writers or potential writers toward their own poems by "using as a springboard the poems of others." It is both an anthology of good contemporary poetry and a book of good, interesting poetry exercises to get you or your students writing poetry. I know of its use in some high school classes, and believe this is a wonderfully appropriate place for this book.

Active Voices II, by James Moffett and Phyllis Tashlik, Heinemann Publishers, Portsmouth, New Hampshire. This fine book rightly calls itself "A Writer's Reader for Grades 7–9," although its activities and value easily could be moved upward in the grades. It offers *many* writing activities in the general categories of: Taking Down (Notation), Looking Back (Recollection), Looking Into (Investigation), Thinking Up (Imagination), and Thinking Over (Reflection). The book's real strength is that it provides copious and very good examples of student work in its activities. A book as good for students as it is for teachers!

On Righting Writing, by Ouida H. Clapp, edited by the National Council of Teachers of English, 111 Kenyon Road, Urbana, Illinois 61801. A good book which includes a number of different activities under the following categories: Getting the Writer Started, Finding a Subject, Developing a Point of View: Sensing an Audience, Sharpening Technique, Writing to Clarify Values, and Exploring Writing Systems. The National Council of Teachers of English has many other publications available for direct classroom application; request a catalogue if you're not already a member.

To Read Literature, edited by Donald Hall, Holt, Rinehart & Winston, New York. Edited (and a good part written by) Donald Hall, himself a poet. This, like the subsequent books listed in this bibliography, will be of literary interest to teachers. In this anthology, Hall divides literature into Poetry, Fiction, and Drama, guides the reader toward distinguishing between good and bad examples of each type of writing, and offers copious and wonderful examples of all. It's a big book (1,300 pages) but not excessive. Included is a guide to literary terms and an appendix entitled "Writing on Writing." Highly recommended as a resource book.

The Art of Fiction, edited by R. F. Dietrich and Roger H. Sundell, Holt, Rinehart and Winston, New York. Another anthology, this one only fiction. Uses short story examples to illustrate Substance, Characters, Actions, Voices, Language, Experiences, and New Directions. Also a good resource book.

You Must Revise Your Life and *Writing the Australian Crawl,* by William Stafford, University of Michigan Press, Ann Arbor. I love these books. By the gentle and revered Oregon poet, these works talk directly about poetry: its process, its directions and indirections, its sources and resources, the teaching of it, the writing of it, and the performing of it. Highly recommended for both writers and teachers.

Technicians of the Sacred, edited by Jerome Rothenberg, University of California Press, Berkeley. Subtitled "A Range of Poetries from Africa, America, Asia and Oceania," this anthology of ancient and tribal poetry is fascinating and powerful. It's another hefty one (500 + pages) and is loaded with poems a teacher can read as examples of chants, incantations, spells, and important events in the lives of humans. There's wild, haunting work in here, much of which can be appreciated—and adapted—by kids.

In the Middle: Writing, Reading, and Learning with Adolescents, by Nancie Atwell, Heinemann Publishers (Boynton/Cook), Portsmouth, New Hampshire. An exciting, optimistic book which may change your teaching life. (It's working on mine.) Using models and philosophies developed by Donald Graves, Donald Murray, Lucy Calkins, and others, Atwell vividly describes a step-by-step "writing workshop" program, which, in conjunction with the reading program she describes, forms a large part of her English curriculum. The book is written in very accessible language; descriptions are sequential. Highly recommended.

Free to Write: A Journalist Teaches Young Writers, by Roy Peter Clark, Heinemann Publishers (Boynton/Cook), Portsmouth, New Hampshire. A very good book, written by a professional journalist who began teaching writing in a classroom and "got hooked." Clark's language is direct, his approach is sound, and his perspective is fresh. The book is practical and eminently usable for the day-to-day teacher. Chapters include Cub Reporters, Writing and Reporting, Writing Every Day, Talking Writing, Growing Writers, Making a Mess, Exploring, Focusing In, Getting Organized, Editing, Publishing Stories, Evaluation and Grading, and Writing

Anxiety. A very sound book, and also highly recommended.

The Discovery of Poetry, by Frances Mayes, Harcourt Brace Jovanovich, New York. I could write twenty pages of paeans to this book. Whether you are a teacher who thinks you'd like to know more about poetry itself in order to teach the reading and writing of it, or whether you are a writer or a specialist teacher of poetry, this book holds manifold wonders. It is a book to be stranded on a deserted island with; a book written by a poet and imbued with a deeply poetic sensibility. But the text is written in plain language and can teach much about the nature of poetry. Examples Mayes cites sometimes are familiar, but often, for me at least, are discoveries to be cherished. I think this book will one day be famous, and I urge you to look at it.

Finally, an urging to look at the work of Donald Graves *(Writing: Teachers and Children at Work: A Researcher Learns to Write),* Donald M. Murray *(Learning by Teaching, Write to Learn, A Writer Teaches Writing),* and Lucy Calkins *(The Art of Teaching Writing, Lessons from a Child: On the Teaching and Learning of Writing).* Each of the three is important in the field of process-oriented writing, and each continues to be a moving force in the changing orientation of writing instruction.

Appendix A: Two Prose Poems

The prose poem, usually a short piece of writing in the form of prose but often having the imagistic and rhythmic characteristics of poetry, is used with increasing frequency by writers these days. Here's one by Russell Edson:

The Family Monkey[1]

We bought an electric monkey, experimenting rather recklessly with funds carefully gathered since grandfather's time for the purchase of a steam monkey.

We had either, by this time, the choice of an electric or gas monkey.

The steam monkey is no longer being made, said the monkey merchant.

But the family always planned on a steam monkey.

Well, said the monkey merchant, just as

---

the wind-up monkey gave way to the steam
monkey, the steam monkey has given way to
the gas and electric monkeys.
    Is that like the grandfather clock being
replaced by the grandchild clock?
    Sort of, said the monkey merchant.

    So we bought the electric monkey, and
plugged its umbilical cord into the wall.
    The smoke coming out of its fur told us
something was wrong.
    We had electrocuted the family monkey.

And the following is excerpted from a much longer prose
poem by Aimé Césaire, a writer from Martinique.

I want to rediscover the secret of great speech
and of great burning. I want to say storm. I
want to say river. I want to say tornado. I want
to say leaf. I want to say tree. I want to be
soaked by every rainfall, moistened by every
dew. As frenetic blood rolls on the slow current
of the eye, I want to roll words like maddened
horses like new children like clotted milk like
curfew like traces of a temple like precious
stones buried deep enough to daunt all miners.
The man who couldn't understand me couldn't
understand the roaring of a tiger . . .[2]

---

[2] From Return to My Native Land, by Aimé Césaire, translated by John
Berger and Anna Bostock (London: Penguin Books, 1969), translation
copyright © John Berger and Anna Bostock, 1969. Grateful acknowledgment is made to Présence Africaine for permission to reprint part of
Cahier d'un retour au pays natal.

Appendix B:
Fifty Contemporary Titles

Caretaker
Hood Ornament
Women Laughing
Hollywood
Death Comes for an Old Cowboy
Picking Cherries
Investigation of a Young Dog
It's Been Good to Know You
The Confession
Thinking of Peas
Plink!
The Beekeeper's Beard
Edges
Magnolia
In Ott's Basement
Russian History Lesson
A Letter Found on a January Night in
    Front of the Public Theater

Taken from back issues of the following magazines: *Pequod, Indiana Review, Black Warrior Review, California Quarterly, Field, The Ohio Review,* and *Webster Review.*

There Go the Sheep
The Adolescent Life on Fire
The Corporal Who Stabbed Archimedes
Anesthetic
A Voice Enters
The Gray Cat
Horse in Early Spring
To William Blake
Schoolhouses
Frozen In
August Birthday
Fur Traders Descending the Missouri:
    1845
Deep Mining
The Two of Them Together
The Blind Always Come as Such a
    Surprise
Groves in East Tennessee
Unfinished
Here
The Blue Dress Shows Skin
January First
Strangely Insane
Working on the Roof
Trees at Dusk
Going Blind
Marie Antoinette
Lizard
Menstruation
Adventures in Heaven
He Died in a Barber Shop
Seeing a Hobbled Horse Cross the Field
That's All Right, Mama
Death of a White-Haired Friend
Not Yet Dark

Appendix C:
Symposium — Censorship

In January of 1989, at Potrero Hill Middle School in San Francisco, a school literary magazine was published. The title of the magazine was *Potrero Hill Beat*.

The publication of a literary magazine in a middle school is a pretty common occurrence. Equally common is the presence of fairly direct language in this publication of writing by students.

What is not common, however, is that the magazine was ordered impounded by the Superintendent of San Francisco Public Schools, Mr. Ramon Cortines. Superintendent Cortines objected to a number of writings contained in *Potrero Hill Beat*; the following story, printed verbatim and written by two eighth-graders, is what seemed to precipitate the magazine's censorship.

Bulldog and Fastass

This is a story about a girl named
Bulldog and her partner, Fastass. I don't
know their real names, but that is what
people called them. They are prostitutes
and the story takes place in Queens, New
York.

Well, it all started out one night
when Fastass and Bulldog went on their
corner to wait for their pimp, Monkey.
Bulldog was wearing a green mini and
orange and white socks. She is over-
weight and also wore blue and white
Nike shoes. Fastass was wearing the
same old tight blue jeans and a white T-
shirt that said MONKEY. So while they
were waiting for their pimp, a car
stopped and a man was in there looking
for hoes. So they got into the car and
drove away till they got to the hotel
room about a quarter to nine. They asked
the man how much money he had He
said he would give them $300 for
everything so they took off their clothes
and began to have sex without a con-
dom. And to top this all off both women
had sex with the same man at the same
time.

The next day the two women saw
their pimp, Monkey. He asked them

where they had been and they gave him his share of the money. About six months later Bulldog and Fastass were feeling sick. They went to the doctor. The doctor detected AIDS and told them they had three months to live. They told their pimp, Monkey, and he said that he would kill them. Bulldog began to cry as he pulled out his black 38 handgun. Just then the police busted in the door and said "FREEZE!"

Then the police told Monkey he was under arrest for attempted murder and they took him to jail. Two weeks passed and Monkey had just got out of jail. He caught Bulldog and Fastass and beat them. As he walked down the street he yelled back "You Bitches!"

About three days later Bulldog began to feel pain all over her body and she began to yell, "Fast, I'm dying. I'm leaving the world now."

After that Fastass was by herself. About two months later, Fastass took a lot of sleeping pills but before that she left a note that said, "I don't have any reason to live so I have just took alot of pills. Because I was going to die anyway of AIDS."

—Rachel Head and Ayanna Gray

That's the story. The magazine, printed at a cost of $2,800, was impounded and put in a school storage room. Those that had already made their way to the library were removed.

The censorship of the magazine hit the local newspapers almost as soon as it happened. There were many news articles and opinion columns written on the issue. The idea that such censorship could occur in San Fancisco, generally a bastion of liberal thought, shocked many and gratified some.

The controversy raged for a week, intensifying as time passed. Finally, Superintendent Cortines allowed the magazine to be distributed. Two days later, the *San Francisco Examiner* broke an unrelated story about teenage prostitution, headlined "Young Hookers and Johns Just Blocks from City Hall."

All of this was *before* the literal condemnation of writer Salman Rushdie for his words in *The Satanic Verses*.

What follows, then, reader, is a symposium in which the censorship of this particular magazine is discussed. Those who have written statements or essays for this section include Superintendent Ramon Cortines of the San Francisco Public Schools; Wendy Coyle, faculty adviser to the *Potrero Hill Beat*; Dorothy Erlich, director of the northern California chapter of the American Civil Liberties Union, student writers, and this writer. It is my hope that these writings will help elucidate some of the many issues involved in the complex concept of free speech — especially as that idea relates to what we encounter in public schools.

The *Potrero Hill Beat* is a magazine containing stories, poems and artwork of students at Potrero Hill Middle School that was published by the staff of Potrero Hill Middle School.

It is my belief that, as Superintendent of Schools, I have a responsibility to ensure that all publications produced by any of our schools are ones of which all the students and parents can be proud.

After reading the Potrero Hill Beat I concluded that this literary work did not meet the above criteria and it is for this reason that I asked that it not be distributed. My initial decision had nothing to do with trying to stifle the right of free expression; it was a sincere effort to continue helping all of our schools to put their best foot forward.

When the issue of censorship was raised I had to agree that in the United States of America that all persons have the right to freely express their viewpoints as long as they are not libelous or obscene. In applying these criteria to the *Potrero Hill Beat* I concluded that the story I objected to did not violate these criteria; thus the school distributed the magazine.

I feel that it is important for adults in providing guidelines for students to discuss the appropriateness of material for a literary magazine in light of the goal of publishing such a work. It is the duty of all school personnel to promote and encourage student writing that is appropriate to the audience for which it is intended; one also needs to consider the age level of the audience. There are many, many stories, poems and works of art that might be appropriate for adults that would not be suitable for young children and teenagers.

The challenge to school personnel today in editing and publishing a literary magazine is to encourage students to submit material that is appropriate so that the publication is one that everyone can be proud of rather than becoming embroiled in a free speech issue.

Ramon C. Cortines, Superintendent of Schools
San Francisco Unified School District
135 Van Ness Avenue, San Francisco, CA 94102

Student Opinions: A Mix

The following essays on the subject of censorship of the Potrero Hill Beat were written by students in my sixth-grade honors English class. I regret that I am not able to print all essays written, but hope that this sampling will give the reader an idea of passion and intensity of belief experienced by students around this issue.

(Parenthetically: there's mention in these writings of "gifted" kids not working on or having work in the magazine. That is a reference to one of Superintendent Cortines's criticisms of the magazine, as reported in the San Francisco Examiner.)

* * *

"Real world"—this is what the children at Potrero Hill Middle School are writing about in their magazine. What is the "Real World"? Condoms, sex, drugs, AIDS, abortion, pregnancy. The kids at Potrero Hill are putting all this in their literary magazine. My opinion about this is that the children are knowing the facts about these things and telling other people these things in their *own way.* The Superintendent of schools was wrong to confiscate the magazine. 700 copies of the magazine were printed. 2,800 dollars was spent to print them. Now all the copies of the magazine are stacked in a school storage room. The children have every right to write those things in the magazine.

—**Dennis Duong**

* * *

246

I think that the Superintendent was correct in withholding the magazine. I don't care about the subjects in the magazine. The stories talk about the real world that we all live in and that is fine with me.

The only reason I didn't like the story was the language. Not that kids shouldn't hear "bad" language; we all hear foul language in and out of school and even let a "bad" word slip out occasionally. It's just that it isn't necessary. Why should words that TV stations blip out in the movies be published in a school literary magazine?

It could also get the school into serious trouble. If a parent were to look at the magazine, they wouldn't even have to read it: the words would catch their eye immediately and they would probably call the school to complain. This could lead to a lot of trouble.

If the editors were trying hard to put out a good magazine then they should have gotten permission from the authors to change the wording and clean up the worst of the bad language. Then I would have thought it was OK to print.

There is one thing I definitely think is wrong. The Superintendent complained that the magazine was not by students in the gifted and talented program. Just because a student is not categorized as gifted or talented, they shouldn't be denied the right to publish a magazine.

—**Erika Christie**

*   *   *

247

Well, my opinion is that the magazine shouldn't be withheld by the Superintendent, but it should have been corrected. A reason for it to be given to the public is that they're just writing about what they think and want to write. It's as simple as that, because if someone wants to write what they think, nobody would go and say don't write that. If they didn't like it, why didn't they just take it out of the magazine before it was printed?

Another reason is that just because one story isn't good, the others don't need to be thrown away, too. It's like if the Chronicle had a bad story then thousands of newspapers would be stored away. It's just crazy. The part when somebody said there was no gifted in the project was dumb, cause he makes kids that are not gifted seem dumb.

It's just what they think and it's so harmful that it could kill? Well, it sounds dumb and thoughtless and I hope you agree with me.

—**Eduardo Chavez**

* * *

My opinion is that Superintendent Cortines has a right to pull out the issue of the Potrero Hill Middle School magazine. I think the students should have left out the foul words. It would have been better. If the students had read the student handbook carefully, they would have known the rule: no foul language!

My opinion is that the students may be able to say foul words to their friends. But in a school literary magazine I don't think it's appropriate. I don't even think they should talk to their friends that way.

It should be embarrassing for the school to know that their students swear and would like the whole world to know it.

Superintendent Cortines is right to pull the magazine out. I think the editor should have looked more carefully at the wording. The editor should have changed it. I think that the teachers should have been surprised at the students.

—Ula Toa

* * *

I feel that the Superintendent was wrong to censor the magazine. To support my opinion, I have a few points to make:

- The first amendment to the Constitution allows free speech and expression of ideas. This law also applies to children.
- It is impossible to hide the real truth about prostitution and drugs, as well as many other issues which are important, yet embarrassing.
- Children seem to learn better from other children about saying, "no" to drugs, about wearing condoms, and other things trying to be taught by the "Just Say No" Campaign and in family life education. Besides, some of the writers may be other students' peers.
- The articles may be about sex, drugs, and swearing, but it seems to me that they all have good morals, whether they teach about AIDS, condoms, drugs, etc.
- Kids will be informed by public news about drugs and sex anyway. The only difference with the "Potrero Hill Beat" is that it is passed around school.
- Although I feel that there should be some representatives from the gifted program, I feel that the regular-level students also have good writing talents.

—Joseph Luk

* * *

I don't agree with the Superintendent, because of free speech. Other kids have a right to know what other kids think about AIDS and prostitution. He shouldn't have taken the story away because we, as Americans, have a right to such free speech as adults in this country.

Those two kids who wrote the story were only writing what they thought was the truth, which was mostly pretty much the truth. It is not like there is no such things as AIDS and prostitution in this world. It's as if everyone is trying to run and hide from the fact that there is AIDS and prostitution around the world or in the country, city, or even your own neighborhood.

We can't hide from these issues forever. These kids have been working hard on that project probably for a long time and have put a lot of effort into it. We need to bring it out into the open for once and discuss it with us so we can learn more of the facts and learn to prevent it from happening to us instead of running away from AIDS and prostitution every time these issues pop up.

I think the Superintendent should let them publish it over, so that the other kids can see what those kids were thinking about AIDS and prostitution. Maybe, just maybe, if we discuss this often, we can prevent more people from getting AIDS and from being prostitutes.

So as I said, the Superintendent should republish the stories.

—**Erica Yee**

* * *

Writings from the Adventures of Life: The *Potrero Hill Beat*

The students at Potrero Hill know so much about life, and they have so much to say. Their myriad backgrounds have produced strong experiences and a poignant wisdom.

Would-be writers have traditionally migrated to New York, to Paris looking for "life" — for experiences about which to write. Be it blessing or curse, our students already possess that "stuff of life." We should validate it, and, for purposes of art, show its blessing: to transmute its pain to literature, poetry, story.

To constantly confront our students in the language arts with their lack of skills is to negate their strengths. Skills are more effectively taught with a "Wow! Look what you know!" perspective.

A fellow educator recently told me that minority students should not write about their lives. "They see enough of that," she said, "they must be challenged to write about other things."

Certainly I agree in reaching out and upward. But when an English assignment requires a student to write about a character in his or her neighborhood and that character is a prostitute or a drug dealer, how can a teacher send the child back to write about the ice cream man? How can the teacher deny the student's reality and voice?

There are those who believe that a diet of inspiring works will uplift. That helps, of course. But coming from cracker-poor mountain isolation or ghetto housing and *saying* you're going to be a doctor doesn't make it so. That statement may please a teacher or provide a goal, but without knowing the environment that shapes us, or knowing that we need a firm psychological ground in reality in order to survive the climb, we simply won't make it. Denying our roots is not a good idea.

The *Potrero Hill Beat* touched these issues. Do we censor and negate the harsh realities that appear in written work? Do we present only the glorified side of achievers? How best do we motivate and keep our students on track, and in school so that they will meet those goals?

I believe that learning to write with depth and feeling, using the adventure of life, is one way.

—**Wendy Coyle,**
Faculty Advisor,
Potrero Hill Beat

A Fragility Worth
Our Vigilance

The specter of a literary magazine being confiscated by public officials is not the image ordinarily conjured up by enlightened San Franciscans. Yet when the magazine in question was published by junior high school students, and the public officials were from the educational establishment, that is precisely what happened

In January of this year San Francisco School Superintendent Ramon Cortines determined that the student writers featured in a junior high school literary magazine, the *Potrero Hill Beat*, who wrote about such urban truths as drugs, gangs, AIDS and prostitution, did not "put the school's best foot forward." The Superintendent ordered all 700 copies of the magazine seized and locked in a store room.

Fortunately a state law and a remarkably courageous journalism teacher combined forces to convince the Superintendent to release the confiscated publication.

It was a victory for the student readers and writers at Potrero Middle School, and an important reminder to all who value free expression and academic freedom. It illustrates that even in the tolerant climate of the Bay Area, the voices of inner-city school students can often be at odds with the censors that lurk among us. The First Amendment is designed to provide protection against just such arbitrary action by government authorities. However, that protection is not necessarily provided to high school students due to a 1988 U.S. Supreme Court decision in the *Hazel-*

wood case which gave school authorities greater power to control school publications.

This limitation under federal law on free expression for public school students does not conform with existing California law, and thus it is largely inapplicable in our state. In California, a state Education Code provision (E.C. 48907) explicitly protects the rights of students to free expression. School officials cannot censor material written by students for school publications unless it is obscene, libelous or slanderous, or likely to incite others to commit illegal or disruptive acts. Even in these instances, such charges must be made through a process which would allow the students an opportunity to seek review of any decision to censor materials.

While one might not expect junior high school students to be well-versed in the fine distinctions between federal and state laws as they relate to school censorship, one *would* expect public officials to act lawfully when carrying out their duties. To insure that public officials were aware of California's law, immediately following the U.S. Supreme Court's Hazelwood decision last year, a Legal Advisory was rushed out to all County and District Superintendents from the General Counsel of the Department of Education. Somehow it appears that this advisory never made its way to Superintendent Cortines's desk.

When Cortines reversed his censorship decision a few days later, possibly when this directive did finally reach him, he still failed to fully understand the limitation on his power to restrain the publication of material, saying "The First Amendment has been a smoke screen. People confuse this with a student newspaper. It is a district document."

Superintendent Cortines is not the first school official to claim authority to censor "district documents," nor
will he be the last. Students such as Hung Dang, whose
poem "Cry Freedom," published in the *Potrero Hill Beat*,
captures a young immigrant's first awareness of the civil
rights movement, are often targets of official censors. Their
comments, school officials say, about issues which deeply
and powerfully affect their lives, are often unwelcome.
They are perhaps too candid, often too street-wise, to sail
safely under the school masthead.

What lessons do students learn from this exercise
when junior high school author Jaime Santamaria is told
that his frightening expression of a tortured drug nightmare does not deserve a forum because it evokes the "wrong
image," according to school officials? Is it that their candor
is unacceptable, their nightmares not worthy of expression,
their life experiences not acceptable for publication? Do
they learn that the values embodied in the First Amendment that they were taught in civics class were meant only
as classroom exercise, not for the real world?

Ayanna Gray, Rachel Head, Hung Dang, Jaime Santamaria, and their classmates were fortunate to have the
respect and support of their journalism teacher, Wendy
Coyle, and the backing of the teachers' union who went
to bat for her students. Moreover, their efforts were wholly
supported by the State Education Code. In school districts
throughout the nation, and in classrooms throughout this
state, current laws rarely require that schools keep faith
with the First Amendment, and teachers do not necessarily
see free expression as consistent with classroom decorum.
On a daily basis students are silenced. Reporters are not
alerted to this injustice, and no defense is waged. Another

generation of student writers are discouraged from taking the risk of expressing themselves.

Even as the death threats against author Salman Rushdie provoke an international outcry against censorship, sometimes it takes a smaller incident, like the confiscation of the *Potrero Hill Beat,* to remind us that the rights of students and the right to free expression are extraordinarily fragile ones, which require constant vigilance and deserve consistent protection.

> **—Dorothy Erlich,**
> **Executive Director,**
> **American Civil Liberties Union**
> **of Northern California**

Thoughts on the Censorship
of *Potrero Hill Beat*

I like to think that Mr. Ramon Cortines, the Superintendent of Public Schools in San Francisco, censored Potrero Hill Middle School's literary magazine to engender healthy discussion and debate throughout the city.

If that was the intention of this initial decision, he succeeded magnificently. Newspapers seized upon the story, school hallways were the scenes of lively discussion among both adults and kids, and much important critical writing issued from English classes.

Perhaps, though, such good talk and writing was not the superintendent's inspired *sub rosa* agenda. Perhaps he simply and truly didn't want the magazine to see the light of day.

If this is the case, it's easy to jump on the Constitutional bandwagon, glibly mumble something about the First Amendment, condemn the man to a place in history beside Thomas Bowdler, and think no more of the matter.

But for teachers, and for those interested in the specific internal dynamics of an already wildly dynamic public education system, the subject is important, and deserves discussion. The issues are not easy, but there is light enough to guide us.

* * *

O.K. Who started this magazine, and what was it represented to be? The answers are easy enough to determine, but having the answers themselves would do nothing to illuminate the wider philosophical issues of our discussion.

Whoever began the magazine, whether an individual, an English department, an administration, or an entire staff, must have had a specific idea as to what would be published.

The possible categories seem most often to be two: *exemplary* and *representative*.

If the staff at an early point decided on printing *exemplary* work, a move toward the private would need to occur. Private? How?

Reader, if you and I were sent into a grocery store and were asked to return with a fine example of an apple, there's a good chance (assuming that the grocery store had a selection of apples) that we'd return with two different apples.

So in choosing *exemplary* writing, an orthodoxy must be established. In the creation of that orthodoxy, certain wills and tastes prevail. Therefore, even if a few people agree as to what work is worthy to use as an example, the agreement ultimately will be a private one—an imposition of tastes upon readers.

This occurs all the time. It happens in every "professional" literary magazine and in every university literary magazine. It happens in publishing houses. Writing is judged, and accepted or rejected. The motive in these cases is often profit and reputation. Less often the motive is a publication's self-perpetuation. Too occasionally, the motive is excellence.

Let's say that Potrero Hill Middle School wanted to issue an *exemplary* publication. Apparently not all minds—and in a large public school system there are many, at various levels of function and dysfunction—agreed in this case as to what defines a fitting "example" of good student work.

And this precisely is the problem with *exemplary* publications in a place like a public middle school: by the time everyone agrees as to what is "good," a great majority of examples written by *the public* have fallen by the wayside, and what is left reflects the orthodox, often narrow, and almost always specifically inculcated definitions of the Example Choosers.

So it seems true that if, at Potrero Hill Middle School, the chief Example Chooser did not clearly specify to the kids the definition of *exemplary* work, then that adult did a disservice to Rachael Head and Ayanna Gray in allowing them to submit their story to the magazine.

Clearly, then, it's greatly easier and more inclusive in a middle school to create a magazine that's *representative* of student work. While some judgment must certainly remain—and be defined—a magazine *opens* when it moves toward a *reflection* of kids' ideas and work

We are, after all, *public* schools, and much as we'd like to, we can't control what our kids see, hear, think, or (often sadly) live.

Those who can accept that idea—and teach English—urge kids to write from their experience, moving later to fictive possibilities. Nothing new here. Writers throughout this century have exhorted others to "write what they know."

The girls who wrote this story apparently did just that: they wrote what one local columnist called a cautionary tale, and this cautionary tale certainly comes from their realistic perception of the urban world. The work is *representative*: that is, it reflects an only slightly fictive possibility set in a big city in the United States of America toward the end of the twentieth century—just as Dickens (yes, considerably more prolifically and eloquently) described the raw and tawdry urban life of a century before.

And while we shouldn't pretend that this snippet of writing before us will serve to expose our own time one hundred years from now, we can say a few things in admiration.

The first is that in just a few sentences, really, Rachel Head and Ayanna Gray painted a picture that revolted our sensibilities.

That's good?

In this case, I think so, for without writing specifically for shock value or on a peer dare, with a very broad brush they painted a picture of lives indeed sordid and hopeless.

This story *is* a cautionary tale, and we might remember that in English such literature is of our earliest, harking back to the morality plays of the fourteenth and fifteenth centuries. Not one student in the classes to whom I read this story interpreted it as anything other than a warning. They shared my own revulsion of the life and death situations of the prostitutes, and marked well the little parable's lessons. Moreover, one student related what we adults all know and perhaps are too timid to say: that within our public schools there are girls — and boys — who attend school by day and sell their bodies by night. A true horror: a reality.

And of lessons, should the authors not be congratulated for learning what we in the public schools teach in the way of AIDS education? Not only have Rachel and Ayanna taken to heart this lesson, but in writing such a story they have put the lesson into a form likely to be read — and perhaps internalized — by their peers. This is a mature and responsible step. We could say that the possibility exists that this piece of literature might save a life. How often can even a professional writer say that about his or her work?

So if these attributes reflect the *representative* approach to running a school literary magazine, I cast my ballot in that direction. Though I am an English teacher and a writer, I would strongly prefer to publish a piece such as this — understanding fully that I may not be publishing "good literature" — over issuing a droll, eviscerated tome which kids won't read, and, in not reading, won't learn a whit from.

Certainly there can be compromise between tough-stuff and extraordinary writing in a magazine. It seems a matter of being willing to mix works published in the same way kids in our urban schools are mixed: as simple and as complicated as that.

* * *

In discussion of this censorship issue at school, a highly esteemed colleague and long-time English teacher argued passionately that literature should *uplift*, should show the best, should set a high example for students. And in discussing this with other colleagues, I found what seemed a generational difference in attitude toward this idea.

At this writing, I am forty-two years old. My colleague is nearing retirement. Two different pedagogical trainings seem evident here. My colleague, if I have it right, was educated toward literature as having some measure of *prescription*. And, it follows, by virtue of that prescription, that literature can change behavior.

My own training was that literature should be (note the prescription here) *descriptive*, and should mirror, as precisely and as objectively as possible, the lives we live and the physical conditions in which we live them.

Are we so far apart, in so few years? The strangest thing is that this little story, if we squint our eyes and look at it again, tends to bring these two camps together, rather than to divide. For it does both: prescribe and describe — teach a lesson and show the horror from which that lesson issued.

But maybe it is a problem that the language in the story itself isn't exalted, or, again, exemplary. And again the question of defining the *publicness* of a public school arises. And again the question of whether the story is *good literature* arises.

To the latter, I say no: it's not very good literature. By my own (private) standards of what elements make up good writing, it falls far short.

But! This is middle school, not a university. But this is a big city in the most violent country in the world. But this magazine, if it is of the *representative* type, is a cross-section of the school population. (The superintendent decried the fact that the honors classes didn't have work represented; I join him in that, yet feel compelled to point out that this same fact increases the likelihood that the numerical majority of the student body will be represented in what is printed . . .)

So sad it is to say, but what we English teachers often hope for these days is a simple coherent paragraph: a demonstration that one sentence might follow logically from what came before it. This story succeeds in that.

Eloquence? No. For its authors, we hope that comes later. For now, just competence.

Similarly, how grateful the typical middle school English teacher would be to see Rachel Head's and Ayanna Gray's peers *reading* this magazine, this story! Not watching TV, not playing video games, but reading! The printed word!

The salary's abominable, and the little joys are few enough. Let's recognize them!

* * *

A few other issues should be talked about.

One is another interesting complication of the public/private question.

Potrero Hill Middle School has been "adopted" by a major San Francisco corporation. Such adoption means, among other things, that the corporation works in partnership with the school by offering tutoring via company employees, and by financially subsidizing certain programs.

In fact, this corporation paid $2,800 for the printing of seven hundred copies of this controversial issue of *Potrero Hill Beat*.

A perceptive colleague of mine speculated that the superintendent had the issue confiscated because he got a phone call from an adopter-corporation executive:

"What the hell is this we paid for—you're printing stuff like this?"

I don't know if this occurred: one can conjure pictures of a gray-suited executive vice-president who lives comfortably in the suburbs picking up the magazine, its contents completely incomprehensible to him, and calling the superintendent, who, upon hearing the vice-president's complaint, himself conjures pictures of whole trainloads of paper money disappearing forever over the horizon. Over a story of three hundred or so words long?

"We'll pull the magazine."

I like to think that this scenario is preposterous, but it's possible that my colleague's perceptions are not far

265

wrong. Anyone who has worked in an urban district for any length of time knows that the motivations for strange actions are virtually limitless.

What should be of concern, here, though, is the definition of this corporate/government "marriage." If this "innovative partnership" system should expand, we'd do well to have established objective expectations, and appropriate behaviors. And have agreed on them, on a schoolwide basis!

Most certainly the schools need money. Our poverty is obscene. Certainly we need support. But when private and public monies mix, where might one find the line that says, my money, yours? If a teacher, paid by the district, directs a magazine, paid for by a corporation, who calls the shots?

Can academic freedom be compromised here? Without a doubt, and we must be most careful and most definitive.

And on the subject of academic freedom: how is it defined in the San Francisco public schools?

Are there written procedures by which a principal or a superintendent may, without specific consultation, impose a private set of standards upon the faculty and student body?

Most colleges and universities have developed extremely sophisticated, specifically articulated definitions of academic freedom: a teacher's rights, a student's, and an administrator's. Do not the students and employees of the San Francisco public schools—or of any public school system—deserve the same, if not for philosophical reasons, then only to aid their predictive sense of what to expect?

Remember in *Billy Budd*, Melville's Captain Vere?

> *But your scruples: do they move as in a dusk? Challenge them. Make them advance and declare themselves.*

*   *   *

Ah, but the beauty in all this is the First Amendment. Teachers and administrators in the halls, kids in the classes, discussing, debating, agreeing, disagreeing, common on this point, at odds on that, unsure on another, writing . . . it's all worth celebrating, worth feeling joy over.

And of the First Amendment: Do kids have rights? Of course. The same free speech rights as we? Of course. The same responsibilities? Yes!

Which?

My definition of a literary magazine does not include libel or defamatory innuendo. I ask students not to name other students or staff members in any piece of writing—*I'm not interested*—and refuse to consider such.

And since we are public schools, I believe that racist writing and writing that stirs hatred of any individual or group should not even pass the threshold of the main entrance, let alone appear in a school publication.

I understand that that is not strictly what the First Amendment means, but I also understand that there are

267

other constitutional rights to consider, and I understand that we're *teachers.*

Last year a student submitted to our literary magazine an excellent drawing of a Nazi storm trooper. The student staff liked it for its artistry and wanted to include it in the magazine. (A goodly number of this student's other drawings also had been accepted.)

I had problems with this, and spoke with the artist outside of class.

"Do you agree with the Nazis?"

"No—I can't stand 'em!"

I explained that the staff liked the drawing, and wanted to print it, but that I had problems with the message that might be communicated should the storm trooper appear.

"Let me think about this," he said, and asked for the drawing back.

The next day he returned, drawing in hand. At the top of the page, above the Nazi officer, was a finely drawn World War I German biplane; beside the biplane, in bold letters, HISTORY SHALL NOT REPEAT ITSELF!

My dilemma was over, and I was grateful.

But was I wrong in offering that question? My civil-libertarian self tells me I should have kept my mouth shut. My teacher self feels it was the right thing to do—feels I moved that student toward specificity, and the magazine toward definition.

I don't know. My scruples here are in a dusk . . . Had he not made that lucky change, would I have allowed the piece to be printed? I'm not sure, but think so; for that trooper himself reminds us that blood has been spilled, and continues to be spilled, over the ability to speak and write freely. And so if we must err, like it or not, we must err on the side of free speech.

We can throw into the garbage what we disagree with or consider trash. What has been withheld we can never know, much less throw.

* * *

And now, as an almost-poetic postscript to the week-long brouhaha, we hear that the superintendent has reversed himself, and is allowing the magazine to be distributed.

In response to mounting pressure? Who knows? But it seems fitting that this little essay should end in the way it began: optimistically.

By virtue of his title alone, the Superintendent of Schools must certainly be considered one of the city's intellectual leaders. I have faith in that, and in such faith am compelled to state certainly that it was precisely for reasons of the furthering of common thought that Mr. Cortines began, encouraged, and enjoyed this debate.

And now, in reversing himself, he means to teach us something of the nature of circumspection and wisdom.

I enjoy believing that.

—Gerald Fleming

Index

DATE DUE

GAYLORD			PRINTED IN U.S.A.